Rooted in Water

*The Importance of Story to Ecopsychology
and the Beginning of a Practice in Narrative
Ecopsychology*

Tiffany A. Dedeaux

ROOTED IN WATER: THE IMPORTANCE OF
STORY TO ECOPSYCHOLOGY AND THE
BEGINNING OF A PRACTICE IN NARRATIVE
ECOPSYCHOLOGY

This book was written under the
advisement of Lisa Lynch as a graduate
level application project for the
Ecopsychology and Cultural Transformation
focus of the Integrated Studies in
Psychology at Antioch University Seattle.

ISBN-13: 978-1463559625

ISBN-10: 1463559623

*This book is dedicated to
all those who are just now becoming
aware...*

ᚱ

Like water, learning is a process for me. This application project is a result of that process.

Acknowledgements

In gratitude I recognize that under the ground, like water seeping through as inspiration, was Dominga Rosalita who conceived of the *Sea Island Project* that turned into *Rooted in Water: The Gullah Geechee People* documentary. For Rosalita, the project was meant to be part of a larger story and an exploration of her heritage. I was also inspired by my Mother, Daisy, who was not only a victim of the untold story, but the one to quench my thirst. B.J. Bullert and my *Communicating Across Cultures* classmates helped to point out that story was important for communicating cultural differences. Both my wilderness quest families from Rite of Passage Journeys were a part of my realization that story mattered. The learning community from ISP Seminar also helped me along the way by asking questions during my presentations and sharing their own struggles with the process. Diana Cantrell, in particular, gave me food for thought when she noted that people under hospice care seemed more at peace once they told their story.

Down the river, where the ground water from the lake empties into the ocean, I find that my continual movement forward was made possible by the entire Antioch University Seattle staff. In particular, Ann Blake made an impression on me by stating that we were there to join a profession; while Michelle Honey helped me to wade through the deeper waters of paperwork access, retrieval, and collection.

Into the air as water vapor warmed by the brilliant sun, was my spirit thanks to work allowed by B. J. Bullert in *Using Media for Social Change* which helped me to wrap my head around symposium planning and Betsy Geist in *Experience of Place* which gave me a chance to soar among the memories of my Australian outback experience. Of specific importance to the process of this application project was *Applied Ecopsychology* with Patricia Hasbach because it is in this class that I journeyed to visit the Tasmanian tiger during a guided meditation and explored the topic of environmental identity.

Falling to Earth in a rain of ideas was assisted by Lisa Lynch, Ned Farley, and Alexandra Hepburn. These adviser/instructors helped to turn my inspiration into reality. Softening the blow of the fall was Cortney Amundson and Lindsay Cummings who started the program with me, inspired me with their ideas, and could relate to the pain of the process.

In going back to the lake, like water, I am "continually reused" (Ward, 2003, p. 2). As I return to the life from which I came, I would like to acknowledge my husband Mark. I met him after I applied to the ecopsychology program, he joined me on many class excursions, and now I return to him a changed person looking to help create a better world.

Tiffany A. Dedeaux
June 2011

Foreword

Tiffany has been an integral part of my work as a filmmaker. She has been a creative partner in my cinematic quest to excavate, to see and attend to the soul of the world and those whose voices go unheard. I believe that the numinous or the divine resides everywhere, not just in the aesthetically pleasing or the heart-warming. The documentary, Rooted in Water is a testament to this. In the face of great suffering and loss, we have the Gullah Geechee people and their stories. They re-membered their splintered selves by honoring the rituals and traditions of their ancestors; they did not dismantle; they did not die.

I believe that we are all endowed with this propulsion towards wholeness, this ineffable need or drive to remember parts of our individual and collective selves, and telling our stories seems to me, the consummate act of transcendence. Tiffany put it best when she noted that:

> Stories, whatever form they take, are important because they help us to find meaning in our lives and experiences, they help us to deal with tough choices we have to make; they divide, they unite, and they make us whole. Stories remind us of who we were, they inform who we are, and they define who will become. Stories take us to places we have never been, and remind

us of where we used to go. Stories break the silence, alter our consciousness, provide connection, and create a collective. Stories inspire us to do more than we have done. A story is a nod to future generations, a wink to our ancestors, and a nudge to embrace the planet of which we are a part. In the end, story is not just another tool, it is a teacher with the power to heal (to heal, to heal).

Dominga Rosalita
June 2011

Rooted In Water

Table of Contents

Chapter 1: Under the Ground

An Introduction

"Meditate on...water, a practice that can open the indigenous soul in all of us to a deeper understanding of the challenges of our times"

~ Linda Buzzell & Craig Chalquist

This application project focuses on the importance of story in "reconnecting individuals to the Earth" (Antioch University Seattle, 2008). This exploration began with the premise that if story could create a sense of connection to a place, then the knowledge of the importance of story and its intentional use could help to bring about the healing outlined by Theodore Roszak (1992, 2001) in his book *The Voice of the Earth: An Exploration of Ecopsychology.* In this book I will look at the importance of story to ecopsychology and some considerations for a practice in narrative ecopsychology. Narrative ecopsychology, for the purposes of this project, is the study of the impact of story on the human/nature relationship. At the center of this exploration is the creation of a video documentary about slave descendents known as the Gullah Geechee who "are a people of land and of water" and are looking "to tell the story of our people...so that we can begin to understand that we really are brothers and sisters" (APPENDIX B).

Introduction and Statement of Topic and Questions

Story as a connection point in the human/nature relationship began to emerge for me during a wilderness quest. One quester screamed when she nearly stepped on a rattlesnake at the base camp entrance. One by one we not only went to go look at the snake, we began telling the story to those who were not there as if it happened to us. It was in this moment I realized that what we witness becomes a part of our experience, and our experience is our story to tell. Three months later, when a person was sharing something I told her with someone else, I realized that I had become part of her story and that created a lifelong connection. In realizing that story could connect two people, I also began to wonder if story could connect people to the natural world in such a way as to be useful to ecopsychologists.

Theoretical Foundation

Story is significant in that it can connect us to the natural world, and ecopsychologists can intentionally use story to connect us to healing. This can be accomplished by helping us to connect with our ecological unconscious, a child-like sense of wonder, a sense of responsibility for rather than a need to dominate our surroundings, and a recognition that the needs and rights of the planet are just as important as our own (Roszak, 1992, 2001). Story as a means of connection is important because conservation psychologists recognize that experience and relationship with the natural world is what creates an environmental identity. It is this environmental identity that helps people to become "invested" in the

environment to the p(
protect it (Clayton & My

Because "na
is...influenced by knowl
natural environment," it
could be used to inspire r
behavior (Clayton & Mye.
Phenomenology, which involves t
world as it is lived, is a way to
existence as a network of relations
existence continually unfolds" (Fisher, ∠∪∪2, p. 11). What phenomenology brings to the idea of story as a tool for connecting is a way "to find those words that are true to our experience - and...like good poetry effect a shift...bringing us a new awareness or understanding of things" (p. 11).

Literature Review

My initial search of literature dealt with seeking as the African version of the vision quest. Seeking, which I was introduced to in the process of creating the video documentary, is an initiation into a religious community; while a vision quest is a traditionally Native American rite of passage from adolescence to adulthood (Rowland, Moore, & Rogers, 1997, p. 365). My literature review search evolved to include African spirituality so that I could see what the differences and similarities were when I compared them to the belief systems that I had already been exposed to during my

...ter determining that my focus would ...tance of story in connecting people to the ...world, I searched using the keywords 'story,' ...end,' 'myth,' 'connection,' 'relationship,' and phrases such as 'the power of story, 'and 'the importance of story' using the OhioLINK database, the internet, Google Books, and Barnes and Noble. I focused on literature that was published within the last five years in an attempt to include the most recent school of thought, but included material that was recommended by teachers and other students that proved to be relevant.

Methodology

To explore the importance of story in connecting people to the natural world, I chose to put together a creative video documentary project entitled *Rooted in Water: The Gullah Geechee People*. Dominga Rosalita, the director/producer, was given permission and recorded members of the Gullah Geechee Nation in 2003. For my part in a look at the importance of story, I logged the tapes, created a script based on ecopsychological principles, and edited the recordings into a video documentary.

Contributions to Self

Focusing on the importance of story was a way for me to connect my skills as a video editor with how I might contribute to the field of ecopsychology. Inspired by the sense of connection I have felt in the natural world, I have combined my passion for crafting stories, with a field of knowledge that has helped me to better understand myself and my place in this world. For me, this book is the end of that journey and a beginning of a practice in narrative ecopsychology which recognizes that if we meditate on story, like water, we will be opened to a deeper way of knowing.

Chapter 2: Down the River

A Review of Literature

> *"Water, if we understand and respect it, has the capacity to wash away the rigid, inflexible aspects of human behavior that lead to conflict"*
>
> *~ Malidoma Patrice Some*

This chapter begins with the realization that although there is some literature that speaks to the topic of story as a way for people to connect, there were only parts of each book or article I encountered that seemed to address the principles of ecopsychology. As a result of the limited relevant material for my topic, I have chosen to include some items that were either required readings for my courses or recommendations from teachers and students even though they were published outside my initial parameters of five years. My search for literature included the Ohiolink database, Ecopsychology Journal, as well as the internet, Google Books, and the electronic bookstore of Barnes and Noble. I initially searched for "Gullah" and "African Spirituality" in hopes of finding more specific material to relate to the video documentary titled *Rooted in Water: the Gullah Geechee People*. As I shifted from wanting to explore the spiritual aspects of their relationship with the land to wanting to explore how their story could impact others, I began another search.

After a search using the phrases "the importance of story" and "the power of story," I went through all references to "story," "stories," "narratives," "myth," "case study," "account," and "connection" that were listed in the books that I acquired as a result of my coursework. After my initial search and textbook review, I watched and transcribed several Ted Talk presentations that either dealt with story or were from their storytelling theme. This final search was a way for me to make sure that I looked at all content relevant to the importance of story that I would not have been sensitive to prior to laying the groundwork for this exploration. By the end of my search for appropriate material – even if I had to pull only a single idea out of one reading – I had 40 pages of quotes and notes to choose from. My thinking about the importance of story was expanded to consider ideas like "modern clinical medicine would not exist if it were not for people's stories which are referred to as case studies" (Dossey, 2009, p. 309). I was touched by the exploration of the importance of story in the life of an assistant professor whose family hid behind silence in order to deal with death, only to find out that "we begin to heal as we story light into shadow, as we story Despair into hope, as we story Life into Meaning, as we story Dream into Daylight" (Poulos, February 2006, p. 115). Still, the reading that resonated most with me was *The Power of Myth* with Joseph Campbell (1988), because it not only explored the importance of myth, it explored its use in the past and how it should be used in the future to connect us to the planet as a whole.

Review of the Literature

In laying out this review, I will 'set the stage' by looking at some different types of story, followed by a look at the themes of 'creative action' that explore why story is important. I will then follow the 'direction the energy is flowing' in order to include the connections and experience that are brought about by story. Throughout this entire review I will share parts of the stories of my life that have made this topic real for me. After nearly two months of reading, reviewing, and organizing my thoughts, I had the sense that I was not done with this line of inquiry and this turned out to be true. This review is specifically about the importance of story to ecopsychology. My work here, as I will explain later, inspired me to define and begin to establish guidelines for a practice in narrative ecopsychology. Before I share with you my inspiration for a practice involving story, people, and place I believe it is important to travel down the river of story.

Setting the Stage

Armed with the resonating idea that Earth warrants its own consideration because of a song I used in a documentary, and a sense of connection I felt with a person during their rite of passage journey, I began to realize that there is power and connection in story. The power of story is present whether I am the person telling the story or receiving the story. The need to share stories came to me when I was finally told the name of my great grandfather. Finding out the name of a family member is the latest in a long list of stories my relatives have not willingly shared because of perceptions they wanted to maintain, privacy, or because they thought the rest of us knew. Unfortunately the stories my family has not willingly shared involve details ranging from the seemingly harmless to important such as hereditary illnesses and lineage. Knowing that I wanted to put together a documentary while I wrote this book, I wondered if the story of a native people, such as the Gullah Geechee, could connect us to them as well as to the land they inhabited. The Gullah Geechee people descend from West Africans who were brought over to be enslaved. Most of the Gullah Geechee people who maintain their traditions live along the southeastern coast of the United States from North Carolina to Florida. *Rooted in Water*, the video documentary, more specifically takes place in a few areas in Georgia and South Carolina. I suggest that if story can connect you to a people and a place, than story can be a tool for the ecopsychologist to connect us to the planet, leading to the healing we seek.

According to Gary Ferguson (2009), a lot of cultures would send their young people to storytellers if they did something wrong. "The storyteller would sit down with them face-to-face...and slowly, carefully begin unraveling this tale or that...[until]...a kid could...claim part of that story as his own" (p. 29). As I compiled this manuscript I realized that those who take this role seriously, consider story to be medicine so that they realize "when to tell a story, which story, and to whom" (Pinkola Estes, 1992, 1995, p. 507).

I experienced the importance of knowing when and to whom to tell a story, and which story to tell, when I walked to examine the solo site of a couple of seekers as an apprentice wilderness quest guide. Trying to impart wisdom, I shared a story of disappointment regarding my own site selection, thinking it would benefit the female quester rather than the male with whom I was walking. In the end, after a series of circumstances, it was the male quester that needed to hear my story. I knew disappointment was a story that needed to be told but I missed when to tell it and to whom it should have been told. Because "as the story is forming, its meaning is not always clear," (Schaefer, 2006, p. 117) it became important to me to not only look at the different forms of story, but in how it has been used to help people to heal.

Defining Story

'Story,' like 'history,' comes from the Latin word 'historia;' which suggests that when we do not share our story "we...sever our links to the past" (Dossey, 2009, pp. 311-312). As story is "an account of...people and events" (Oxford University Press, 2011,

p. 1), not sharing our story means that there are people and experiences that could be lost to future generations. If you consider that "story is far older than the art and science of psychology, and will always be the elder in the equation no matter how much time passes," (Pinkola Estes, 1992, 1995, p. 20) then story is not so much a tool for an ecopsychologist but a teacher that reminds us to respect our elders.

Story in education.

Story in the realm of education – be it narratives, storytelling, critical incident analysis, scenarios, or case studies – "can capture the holistic and lived experience" of what is being taught and "form new and meaningful connections between existing areas of knowledge" (Moon & Fowler, 2008, p. 232). For me, even reading a report that did not confirm whether the stories used were true shifted my perspective because my presumption was that they were true. Jenny Moon and John Fowler (2008) used story to make two points: that the story allowed for a chance to see "different possibilities for development," and that "the very act of telling has educational value and may be more significant than the content" (pp. 233, 234). For at least one student in a class on healing narratives, story "had such an impact" that the she admitted she might not remember a certain procedure from her medical training, but suspected she would always remember a story that taught her that "healing is not black and white" (Sierpina, Kreitzer, Mackenzie, & Sierpina, 2007, p. 629). If a story can remind a medical student that healing might have shades of gray, then it is possible that the story of Wangari Maathai (2010) and the Green Belt Movement of replanting trees in Kenya might remind us that "none of the healing is automatic; it will require much work, for the wounds that have been created in the earth are deep" (p. 16).

The Story of Myth

According to Joseph Campbell (1988), "myths...are...[archetypal] dreams...[that] deal with great human problems" (p. 19). The term archetype "refers to psychological patterns that appear throughout human experience and can be seen in the motifs of age-old myths, legends, and fairy tales" (Aizenstat, 1995, p. 94). As patterns in human experience that address the problems we face, sharing myths with younger generation can be seen as preparing them for adulthood.

While myths are also defined as "a traditional story, especially one concerning the early history of a people or explaining some natural or social phenomenon" (Oxford University Press, 2011, p. 1), Marquetta "Queen Quet" Goodwine thinks that referring to the stories of enslaved West Africans as legends means we are not recognizing how important these stories are to our present and "how knowing those things can take you firmly into the future" (Appendix B).

According to Campbell (1988) myths themselves serve four functions: (1) the "mystical function" of helping a person to realize "what a wonder the universe is;" (2) the "cosmological dimension" of "showing you what the shape of the universe is" with mystery still intact; (3) the "sociological" function of "supporting and validating a certain social order; (4)and "the pedagogical function of "how to live a human lifetime under any circumstance" (pp. 38-39).

Case Study

Stories, whether or true or not, "provide insights into the nature of consciousness and how it manifests in the world," which is why "physicians spend [their] lives listening to stories" (Dossey, 2009, p. 309) that they call case histories. If you think about it in terms of case studies or histories social work professor Brene Brown (2010) says that "stories are just data with a soul" while psychologists Robert Liebert and Lynn Langenbach Liebert (1998) think stories "provide rich, detailed accounts of significant events in an individual's life" and "allow psychologists to explore the richness and complexity of human personality" (pp. 39, 70, 31). By allowing the exploration of personality and providing richer information to psychologists, story is not just a teacher but a means of navigation. Another reason why stories should be shared is because case studies sometimes support the theories of a psychologist, and as a result do not "belong only to the professional subjects, but can be part of any discipline [that] has practical implications for people and their lives" (Moon & Fowler, 2008, p. 235).

Narrative.

The narrative approach is a "special type of case study," or "life history," that "uses the descriptions provided by subjects" which, although biased, provides "valuable information about the person" in terms of "how particular people perceive their lives and which events are recalled, elaborated on, or suppressed" (Liebert & Liebert, 1998, p. 41). Considered "reflexive," the life narrative is a way for us to "both tell and create our reality through our stories, and these stories influence what others believe about us and the actions that are available to us in the future" (Davis C. S., December 2006, p. 1231). Narratives are "a spoken or written account of connected events" (Oxford University Press, 2011, p. 1).

The narrative "helps to connect us with our own and others' humanity" because "we are storytelling animals," as it is "the way we define ourselves, make sense of our world, learn about ourselves, share our experiences, and form group identities" (Sierpina, Kreitzer, Mackenzie, & Sierpina, 2007, p. 627). If we see story as part of our nature as storytelling animals, than sharing a story is intimacy. By serving "as a lifeline to experiencing our own humanity, as well as a bridge that connects us to others," narratives are "an effective antidote to isolation, callousness, and numbness" (p. 630).

Creative Action

The middle part of this journey explores why story is important and what new information comes from the creative use of story. If we look at "the telling and hearing of myth, traditional, and modern tales [as] a means by which we learn what it is to live in our present society" (Moon & Fowler, 2008, p. 234), and we think of stories in terms of "social performances" (Davis C. S., December 2006, p. 1229), we can begin to see that the value of "oral tradition...is the value of relationship" (LaDuke, 2006, p. xi). What allows story to connect us is the relationship it creates. In oral traditions, stories are learned "through assimilation, through living in its proximity with those who know it" (Pinkola Estes, 1992, 1995, p. 505), through relationship. Because story passes from teller to listener I would consider it a 'human between' because "it is not what happens within an individual, but between individuals that makes us human" (Kim & Park, 2006, p. 38). In looking at story as relationship, and considering that "human relationships...form the basis of all healthcare," care that aims to heal as ecopsychology does and is relationship-centered provides "more focus on the psychosocial while simultaneously increasing the probability that the care will be effective, humane, ethical, compassionate, culturally competent, and more satisfying for both patient and provider" (Sierpina, Kreitzer, Mackenzie, & Sierpina, 2007, p. 627). In other words, story can connect people to the natural world by creating a sense of relationship. A practice that is centered on the human/nature relationship will lead to a sense of responsibility and recognition of mutual rights.

Meaning

In considering that mythology "is the relationship you develop between who you are – or who you potentially are – and the infinite world" (S. Kapur, personal communication, November 2009), the stories that we tell ourselves and our children can greatly impact who they are, who they become, and their relationship with earth. Just as there is a difference between a boy who grows up in the Andes and one who grows up in Montana, you would be "profoundly different" – with a different relationship to a place – if you were told as a child that the "mountain is a...Spirit that will direct [your] destiny" than if you were "raised to believe that a mountain is a pile of rock ready to be mined" (W. Davis, 2003). This idea demonstrates that "meaning does not exist by itself" (Liebert E. , 2000, p. 173). While "a tree may flourish apart from us"(p. 173), the meaning of that tree does not. The meaning of the story also does not exist apart from us, because "we make sense of the world in relation to what we know already...[and] in reading a story, we are making meaning from our reading by matching it to our own inner experiences" (Moon & Fowler, 2008, p. 233).

Boundaries

The stories we tell not only affect our relationship with ourselves and the place we inhabit, they can also affect our relationship with each other. The writings of John Locke can be seen as creating a divide between people when you consider him to be "the beginning a tradition of telling African stories in the West" that saw "sub-Saharan Africa as a place of negatives, of difference, of darkness, of people who...'are half devil, half child'" according to one African storyteller (C. Adichie, 2009). If we look at the Africa/West divide as a metaphor for the human/nature divide, "boundaries are of our own making, and...can and should be reconsidered for each new discussion, problem, or purpose" (Meadows, 2008, p. 99). By recognizing that in this "single story" there is no possibility of finding similarities between Africans and the West, just as there is "no possibility of human equals" if all you know of Africa is "a place of beautiful landscapes, beautiful animals, and incomprehensible people...unable to speak for themselves and waiting to be saved by a kind white foreigner" (C. Adichie, 2009). A 'single story' is created when you "show a people as one thing, as only one thing over and over again" until that is "what they become"...a stereotype(C. Adichie, 2009). If the boundaries between people and place are of our own making because of the stories we tell, then changing the stories we tell can change the boundaries we perceive between people and the natural world.

Wholeness

If "the goal of healing is to return the patients to 'wholeness'" (Schaefer, 2006, p. 190), getting them to tell their story would help when you consider "the original definition [of courage] was to tell the story of who you are with your whole heart" (B. Brown, 2010). Story helps to heal because "as humans, we find meaning in our life stories by seeing our lives as coherent wholes" (Davis, 2006, p. 1222). When it comes to self-knowledge, ecopsychology reminds "us of what our ancestors took to be common knowledge: there is more to know about the self, or rather more self to know, than our personal history reveals," (Roszak, 1998, pp. 2-3) because the story of one person "cannot be studied separately from the setting or its history" (Davis C. S., December 2006, p. 1223). As ecopsychology recognizes that we are one part of a larger story, "in the ecological movement, there is [also] the need to think not only in terms of days and years, but also in terms of generations" (Drengson & Devall, 2008, p. 104).

Generational Amnesia

According to Peter H. Kahn, Jr., Rachel L. Severson, and Jolina H. Ruckert (2009) environmental generational amnesia suggests that "by adapting gradually to the loss of actual nature and to the increase of technological nature, humans will lower the baseline across generations for what counts as a full measure of the human experience and of human flourishing" (p. 37). I would suggest that the same idea – generational amnesia – can be applied to story as well, and recorded by ethnographic researchers who take "the opportunity to live amongst those who have not forgotten the old ways; who still feel their past in the wind; touch it in stones polished by rain; taste it in the bitter leaves of plants" and in doing so, recognize that "every language is an old growth forest of the mind...an ecosystem of spiritual possibilities" (W. Davis, 2003). With generational amnesia, when we consider that "culture is a reaction to nature and this understanding of our ancestors is transmitted generation to generation in the form of stories, symbols, and rituals" (D. Pattanaik, 2009), we lose this understanding – and this connection – when the stories are not shared. Children without the understanding of their native land and culture will not have the same connection to that place or to the generations, so that they "don't know where they've come from and so don't have any way of knowing where they are heading" (Schaefer, 2006, p. 154); creating an entirely new lost generation. In this context, to share a story is to save our children from disconnection to their human and natural families.

People have psychological as well as physical needs, and "the ways in which indigenous cultures meet these needs" is through "ceremonies, rituals...music, dancing, telling stories, and making artifacts" (Newman & Jennings, 2008, p. 106). Confidence comes from a sense of meaning and belonging through traditions which help people feel "part of an endless flow that links their ancestors with their descendants" (p. 106). Story is a university with the purpose being "to discover and preserve knowledge and pass it on to new generations" (Stewart & Bennett, 1991, p. 15). The songlines of Australian aboriginals are an example, as they are "information about place stored in the form of songs that are learned from childhood, which can be sung to reveal features of the countryside...layers of information...about a place and the journey through it"

(Newman & Jennings, 2008, p. 154). Another example could be the "spiritual form of songs...[that] allowed slaves [from West Africa]...to maintain a vital link to the inter-connectedness of an older world order" (Johnson, 1998, p. 7). Just as "these cultures focus on learning the story of the land and its patterns in order to relate to it properly" (p. 104), I believe that with story as the teacher, ecopsychology could help to address environmental generational amnesia by opening "access to the ecological unconscious," which is the "path to sanity" (Roszak, 1998, p. 5).

Technological story.

In the information age it would seem that "there is no corner of nature...that does not appear in intimate proximity on television screens" or in pictures (Brody, 2000, p. 288). It is because of this "new kind of relationship...between humans and the rest of nature" that photographers and scientists could be considered the "shamans of our age, making revelatory journeys into places where, in the course of ordinary life, the rest of us cannot go" (p. 288). This new kind of relationship with technological nature – where "technologies...mediate, augment, or simulate the natural world" – can create an "ever-increasing closeness to the natural world" (Kahn, Severson, & Rockert, 2009, p. 37) as it "influences our sense of the dividing line between human and animal" (Brody,

2000, p. 288). By the same token, "movies...might be our counterpart to mythological re-enactments," but without the "sense of responsibility" that is generally put into initiatory rites (Campbell & Moyers, 1988, pp. 102-103).

One way "the technological genius of our species" (Roszak, 1998, pp. 6, 7) can be used in a "life-enhancing measure," is in the creation of a myth, or a series of myths, that "will identify the individual not with his local group but with the planet" (Campbell & Moyers, 1988, p. 30), inspiring us to "rededicate ourselves to reducing the cloud...over our planet" (Maathai, 2010, p. 51). In creating a myth that deals with "how to relate to this society and how to relate this society to the world of nature and the cosmos," we just might realize that we are "an organ of the larger organism" and that "when we say 'save the earth' we're talking about saving ourselves" (Campbell & Moyers, 1988, pp. 41, 90, 228). By identifying ourselves with the planet we are not only recognizing that the planet has equal rights which might help us to shift boundaries so that we also recognize that we are evolving with the rest of the cosmos (Roszak, 1992, 2001, p. 119).

Silence is not always golden.

Christopher Poulos (2006) and his family repeatedly experienced death until they found themselves no longer speaking "of the events that shaped" them (p. 101). That family came to realize that they could release their grief through the telling of the WHOLE story, and that WHOLE story was not just how a person died, because "death is just one small moment" (p. 111).

The impact of the healing narrative is in "acknowledging illness and dealing with it, rather than trying to shove it to the back of your mind where it will only get worse" (Sierpina, Kreitzer, Mackenzie, & Sierpina, 2007, p. 629). Although silence could have "a sacred quality," for this family, "the silence that had protected us now threatened to destroy us" because it was "a dark silence, a silence of truths unspoken and stories untold" (Poulos, February 2006, pp. 102, 107). Cultures can also be threatened by silence when people fail to "bring back the stories of their heritages, preserving them, saving them from death by neglect" (Pinkola Estes, 1992, 1995, p. 511). With elders "dying every two weeks," according to anthropologist Wade Davis, cultures are also threatened when you are "the last of your people to speak the language" and you have "no way to pass on the wisdom of the ancestors"(W. Davis, 2003).

As certain knowledge and stories becomes "as buried streams...buried by disuse," it may be gone, but not forgotten as "nothing was ever lost in the psyche" (Pinkola Estes, 1992, 1995, p. 83). The cultural web of life – the "ethnosphere" – includes "the sum total of all thoughts and dreams, myths, ideas, inspirations, intuitions brought into being by the human imagination, since the dawn of consciousness" (W. Davis, 2003). If stories that are not shared are still around, at least unconsciously, what is lost is the human legacy "of all we are and all we can be" (W. Davis, 2003) because there is no one left to help us make sense of the stories we know.

The Direction the Energy is Flowing

Bill Moyer (1988) felt that listening to Campbell made it impossible not to realize "one's own consciousness stirring of fresh life" or the "rising of one's own imagination" (p. xvi). The stories Campbell would tell of primal societies made Moyer feel as though he were "transported to the wide plains under the great dome of the open sky, or to the forest dense, beneath a canopy of trees," until he "began to understand how the voices of the gods spoke from the wind and thunder, and the spirit of God flowed in every mountain stream, and the whole earth bloomed as a sacred place – the realm of mythic imagination" (p. xviii). The reaction Moyer had to the myths Campbell told demonstrates the direction the energy is likely to flow with the creative use of story. This entire project is also a demonstration of the flow of energy because it was inspired by my own reaction to a documentary I put together entitled *One Voice, One Love, One Spirit: A Sacred Gathering* (2004). I will not cite direct quotes from the video but you can find the source in my list of references. In *One Love* a singer wondered if "the good in man [had] expired" because we were "stealing all the love and the beauty from the land." Because I was unknowingly brought to a new level of consciousness with the suggestion that a shaking earth is "mother nature with a crying heart," I am now exploring if I can knowingly increase my awareness.

Consciousness

If the "whole living world is informed by consciousness" (Campbell & Moyers, 1988, p. 18) and story is a means of transferring information, it stands to reason that story can help transfer consciousness as well. If "only experiences that profoundly alter our view of nature...can empower people to commit themselves to the prodigious task before them," then "therapeutic methods must be powerful enough to shift the ground of our being so that we experience the Earth in its living reality" (Mack, 1995, p. 284).

An example of how a story could lead to actual experience can be found in the science of certain diseases as "legendary figures whose names have become attached to classic diseases didn't stop when they heard stories of illness from their patients," but they continued to collect proof, run tests, and be in the perpetual search "for similar cases" (Dossey, 2009, p. 311).

Connection and the Collective Story

Connection is said to be "what gives purpose and meaning to our lives," and "in order for connection to happen, we have to allow ourselves to be seen"(B. Brown, 2010). Those who demonstrate having connection, had it "as a result of authenticity" and their willingness "to let go of who they thought they should be in order to be who they were" (B. Brown, 2010). Those who did not experience connection, did "fear that [they were] not worthy of connection" (B. Brown, 2010). It would seem, based on this research, that if ecopsychology is to weave a sense of planetary responsibility into "the fabric of social relationship and political decisions" (Roszak, 1998, p. 6), it would have to assist in producing a connection by first alleviating the fear of unworthiness.

As nature and human are said to be kin, and storytelling is an essential family-making praxis, then in the family of the natural world, "stories are vibrant and critical communication events that produce family culture, define family history, feature family uniqueness, develop identity, and display and establish family values" (Poulos, 2006, p. 113). Stories as a means of connection are used in Australian cities because officials see "the way that the sharing of stories can bring people together and help them shape new collective stories" as well as be "a catalyst for change" (Newman & Jennings, 2008, p. 154). The River celebration in Brisbane demonstrates that "to engage properly with a place" we need to engage with "all of the stories of that place"(C. Adichie, 2009). Personally I felt I had an incomplete experience in Brisbane because I did not understand why the city hosted such a large community event to celebrate the river until I read the work of Newman and Jennings.

Experience

Stories of the earth can help to create a connection and a desire to want to care for it, but the inspired interaction with nature is still important so that you do not "detach yourself completely from the reality of nature" (Maathai, 2010, pp. 32, 62-63). Even in the last fifty years "scientists working with the soil...told the rest of the world of the mounting evidence of drastic changes to the earth" after collecting data from the natural environment directly; making it important to have an "experiential learning" component to education because if students "never plant a tree...they may never rediscover the lost sacred groves" (pp. 32, 62-63).

Connection to Water

The Hopi consider water to be our first foundation of life because "we live in water in our mother's womb" (Schaefer, 2006, pp. 146-7). It is in considering the water in the womb of our mother that we can make the connection to Earth as Mother because the planet "has the same percentage of water as the human body does," as if water is "the blood of our Mother Earth" (pp. 146, 7). The human connection to water continues with experiments that show that "molecules of water are affected by the thoughts, words, and feelings of human beings" (Romano McGraw, 2007, pp. 195, 196), which seem to be nothing more than vibrations. Like water, animals also respond to human vibration because when it is low they "reflect our own level of consciousness and expectation" and are "merely...there with us, performing their usual ecological functions" (Redfield, 1997, p. 219). When human vibration increases, "the actions of...animals...become ever more synchronistic, mysterious, and instructional" (p. 219). In considering that human beings are "quantum amplifiers," what we choose, believe, and pay attention to then "has the potential to alter reality," explaining why "the reality you experience has a lot to do with the ideas [you] have been exploring" (Romano McGraw, 2007, p. 197).

Conclusion

As we come to acknowledge that we are "a conscious, self-aware species, we can choose to amplify this shift in consciousness and feel empowered by accepting a life-generating role in the story that demonstrates the healing power of engaging in the Great Work" (Buzzell & Chalquist, 2009, p. 274). By acknowledging the shift and in engaging in the work it is important to know not only that "stories matter," but "many stories matter," so that we realize that a story has the power to "dispossess and to align...to empower and to humanize...[to] break the dignity of a people...[and] repair that broken dignity"(C. Adichie, 2009). Stories "nourish connections between people and the land so that there is a sense of participation in a meaningful cosmos" (Newman & Jennings, 2008, p. 106).

Stories, whatever form they take, are important because they help us to find meaning in our lives and experiences, they help us to deal with the tough choices we have to make, they divide, they unite, and they make us whole. Stories remind us of who we were, they inform who we are, and they define who we will become. Stories take us to places we have never been, and remind of us of where we used to go. Stories break the silence, alter our consciousness, provide connection, and create a collective. Stories inspire us to do more than we have done. A story is a nod to future generations, a wink to our ancestors, and a nudge to embrace the planet of which we are a part. In the end story is not just another tool, it is a teacher with the power to heal.

Discussion

It is at the end of my survey of literature that I conclude that the story of a native people can connect us to their land, but it depends on the story, the teller, and the listener. For the ecopsychologist, story is one part of the process that can serve to connect people to their place, their place to the planet, and the people and planet to healing. What I have learned from this review is that the layers of story are many, and the power of story is so mighty, that it is important to share both with a mindfulness of the medicine you are administering, but also with the sense of responsibility that comes with any power. If we respect story as if it were medicine it could, like water, wash away the boundaries that led to disconnection in the human/nature relationship.

For the Gullah Geechee, the people at the center of the *Rooted in Water* documentary, the story of their ancestors coming over on slave ships is what roots them in water. Knowing their story is what washes away any boundaries that may have existed between them and their kin, Mother Africa, and the land they now call home. This literature review helped me to filter my focus so that I was not only looking at story as a means of connection, but at each story as part of a whole. The whole story of the Gullah Geechee is not just about being kidnapped and enslaved, it is about being brought over as the first cowboys and recognizing that if the animals can learn to live together so can we. The whole story of the Gullah Geechee includes struggles with disconnection as ancestral land has been taken or given away and languages have been lost to assimilation.

This book is unique in the context of the field of ecopsychology because of the story of the Gullah Geechee people, the documentation of their original way of pouring libations as a "gesture of a soul acknowledging the source of all life" (Some, 2009, p. 252), and how they recognize and work to address their own disconnection from both the natural world and their ancestral heritage. They recognize that "the Gullah Geechee culture is good for everybody" because they see the need to move into the future while establishing themselves as the roots "that hold up the tree" (Appendix B).

Chapter 3: Into the Air

Theoretical Orientation

> *"[Water] can purify our souls, restore our ability to attain flow and create magic, and cleanse our genius so it shines brightly"*

> *~ Malidoma Patrice Some*

The goal of this chapter is to explore the influence of ecopsychology as the theoretical foundation of this project and my evolution as a student. When I began my coursework I focused on becoming a wilderness quest guide as well as being involved with a wilderness therapy practice. I will begin this chapter with why ecopsychology is my theoretical foundation, what I understand about ecopsychology, and how my studies had informed this understanding. I will end this exploration by looking at the influence ecopsychology has had on this project.

Why Ecopsychology and How did it Inform my Evolution?

When I began the *Ecopsychology and Cultural Transformation* program at Antioch University in Seattle, I knew that I wanted to be a guide. A broken heart led me to the red centre of Australia where a tour guide encouraged me to let the breeze of the outback caress my cheek while he filled my ears with aboriginal dreamtime stories. I emerged from my Australian adventure feeling divinely connected, and the study of the human/nature relationship has helped me to understand why. Ecopsychology was not chosen to be the theoretical foundation of my work so much as it insisted on its inclusion. Because ecopsychology invites us to "hear the Earth speaking through our pain and distress, and listen to ourselves as if we were listening to a message from the universe" (Macy & Young Brown, 1998, p. 49), I felt a resonance deep within me and knew that this coursework was a river, a threshold, I had to cross.

I committed whole heartedly to ecopyschology during my first few quarters, and knew when I emerged from my own rite of passage journey that this was meant to be a "life-long study, a reciprocity with the natural world in which its depths are as endless as [my] own creative thought" (Shepard, 1995, p. 30). It is this sense of reciprocity, of exchange, that has lead ecopsychology to be the foundation of this project as well. When I looked back, the principles of ecopsychology seemed to reward my steps deeper into the field of study with resonating ideas and affirmations that refused to let me veer off course. In fact, the deeper I waded into this project the more I heard the principles echoed in the words of William Green III, manager of the Gullah Grub restaurant: "we lost all connection with the environment which really was a beacon; it was one of the things that helped keep us down to earth" (Appendix B). What I know as a result of this project, my practicum, and the reflections allowed by my coursework, is that the elements of what will be my ecopsychological practice are the same ones that inspired me to be a guide in the first place: story, people, and place.

What Do I Understand About Ecopsychology?

I understand ecopsychology to be an examination of people, place, and system. It is the study of the human animal, its relationship to its habitat, and the understanding that the human animal and habitat are parts of a whole interrelated system of existence. What draws me to being a wilderness quest guide as an application of ecopsychology is the balance of spirit and science, of the part and the whole, of feeling and experience.

I recognize that by balancing spirit and science "writings on ecopsychology have been criticized for a lack of scientific objectivity" because works tend to reference "concepts like spirituality and indigenous wisdom that are difficult to define clearly" (Clayton & Myers, 2009, p. 10). I also see ecopsychology as part of a larger whole because it existed in some form or fashion before Theodore Roszak (1992, 2001) coined the term. In fact, Roszak considered Paul Shepard to be "the first thinker in the environmental movement to apply psychological categories to our treatment of the planet" (p. 327). As a result of this admission I have pictured ecopsychology as a branch of a tree whose trunk was psychology and whose roots included ecology, philosophy, and environmentalism. The visual image of ecopsychology as a branch also works when you consider that it is meant to reach beyond psychology and recognize that "at its deepest level the psyche remains sympathetically bonded to the Earth" (1995, p. 5) to the extent which "we cannot be studied or cured apart from the planet" (Brown, 1995, p. xxii). In terms of ecopsychology balancing both 'feeling and experience' and 'the part with the whole,' I imagine 'feeling' as being able to reach down deep beyond what we know into the unconscious, into the collective. It is from that depth of the unconscious and the collective that resonance emerges. With the individual and the collective as a patient, ecopsychology can help to restore and enhance harmony and well-being by recognizing that "the goal of healing" is "to return the patient to 'wholeness'" (Schaefer, 2006, p. 190). The attempts to return a patient to wholeness, in the case of wilderness therapy as a means of applying ecopsychology, means recognizing that "a variety of psychological symptoms" are resolved when a person is connected to the natural world "whether through gardens, animals, nature walks outside, or nature brought indoors" (Chalquist, 2009, p. 70). It is through a relationship with the natural world that "one develops a sense of self that is both transpersonal and ecological" and, as a result will lead to "care for the earth without being morally persuaded to do so because one will identify with it as Self" (Fisher, 2002).

Concepts That Attract Me

I am attracted to ecopsychology and the ideas put forth by Roszak (1995) because nature is seen as "alive, active, and capable of communicating with us" (p. 295), which both stimulates me intellectually and represents my own experiences. It is in recognizing that nature is alive that I have come to see that "animals [are] powerful metaphors for stretching beyond...passive position" and "drawing on outer and inner 'wild nature' as a source of personal power" (Cahalan, 1995, p. 223). In considering that nature is alive, I have been opened to recognizing that "the power of place is not in the geography, topography, or any other material aspect of location" (Kelly, 1993, p. 108), and that taking a moment to reflect on my life, to experience a place through my senses, and to listen to the stories of a people and the history of the land has created an atmosphere that has allowed personal transformation to take place.

Writers That Attract Me

The first writer that resonated with me in my ecopsychological studies was Steven Harper. Harper (1995), for me, was the first person to write about a wilderness practice that resembled the kind of guiding I was looking to do. Harper knew that for the human/nature connection to take root, a person had to be "willing to be still and open enough to listen" (p. 185).

The second writer to attract me was Robert Greenway (2009) because he not only wrote about a wilderness practice, he also recognized that people would retreat "from villages, from all human contact, for visions, rites of passage, and spirit guidance" (p. 132). Greenway preferred longer trips to shorter ones because trips that lasted weeks rather than days allowed for "real psychological immersion [to] take place" (p. 133). The most impactful thing Greenway did for me was visit with our class. At a time when I was struggling to define ecopsychology for myself, Greenway simplified ecopsychology to the study of the human/nature relationship (R. Greenway, personal communication, January 26, 2010). It felt to me that Greenway also gave us permission to write about what we knew in that moment, even if what we knew later changed (R. Greenway, personal communication, January 26, 2010). The simple definition of ecopsychology as the study of the human/nature relationship helped me to also simplify and filter my focus so that I did not get lost in elaboration. And the idea that I could speak and write with confidence even when I knew there was more for me to learn, helped me to open up and share what I did know in class discussions.

Another impactful writer in terms of wilderness therapy was Gary Ferguson (2009) because he made a case for "compassionate outdoor therapy" (p. xii) in his book *Shouting at the Sky: Troubled Teens and the Promise of the Wild.* Ferguson recognized that the natural world provided an "essential nudge toward the kind of clarity that often eludes people in times of emotional pain" (p. xiii). As a result of my own practicum experience, I also agreed with Ferguson that there is a need for "starting a program in which entire families can jump into the wilderness and work on their stuff" (p. 14).

I was attracted to the work of Andy Fisher (2002) because he saw "how our human psyches are embedded in and nurtured by the larger psyche of nature" (p. 13). Fisher considered ecopsychology to be a radical praxis that, among other things, sought to employ "free, intentional, creative activity directed toward increasing critical consciousness and reconstructing" (2009, p. 61). For Fisher, praxis meant "taking a hard look at our actual historical conditions and then incorporating these into our theory and our practice...which will change over time as new realities and possibilities become evident" (p. 61). Fisher put ecopsychology in the role of creating "the contexts that will help people recover their own nature and experience" while "being respectful of the position from which each person might begin such a recovery" (p. 183). His idea of replacing therapists with elders is something that will play a role in my own practice because as an apprentice guide I smudged a man that was looking to be initiated as an elder and a butterfly landed on my hand. I took this as a sign, a confirmation that I was "to use the power of gentleness to touch the hearts and minds of wounded beings" (Sams & Carson, 1988, pp. 53-54) such as those seeking to be called elder.

Bill Plotkin (2003) is another writer I have been drawn to as he recognizes that "we come to understand that what is reflected by nature is not just who we are now, but also who we could become" (p. 237). We are to enter nature "as a pilgrim in search of his true home" rather than as we used to enter nature – as a "place of danger, self-testing, and self-discovery" (p. 237). I respect the life shift Plotkin went through in order to create his own wilderness practice, *Soulcraft*. I also appreciate his openness because generally what helps me to understand my own experience is being able to witness the process of another person.

Another author I was attracted to was Satish Kumar. Kumar (2009), in his book *Earth Pilgrim*, recognized that "if there is no Earth well-being, there can be no human well-being" (p. 57). It is through the work of Kumar that I saw the ecopsychologist as a pilgrim who perceives "the planet as sacred" and treats earth with "reverence and gratitude, without any desire to possess the world and exploit it for any short term gain" (pp. 12, 13). According to Kumar, "the significant realization of a pilgrimage" is the realization that "the whole of the Earth is a sacred site" (p. 13). The ideas of Kumar tied together two interests that resulted from my coursework: pilgrimages to sacred sites and the idea of being a co- or partner pilgrim who walks with a person into their mental or physical sacred space. It was as a result of my studies and the ideas of Kumar that I began to shift from the idea of being a guide or ultimately being a therapist, to the idea of being a partner pilgrim. By referring to myself as a partner pilgrim, my goal would be to remain open enough to benefit from the journey, while not assuming the responsibility of having any or all of the answers (Liebert, 2000, p. 4).

How Did My Studies Inform my Understanding?

The core classes of the *Ecopsychology and Cultural Transformation* focus at Antioch University Seattle helped me to define ecopsychology. The practicum helped me to find and reflect on the ecopsychological vision for my life. The elective part of my studies challenged me to fit what I knew of ecopsychology into molds that were not prefabricated. Aside from what I have already mentioned, the classes that have had the greatest impact on what I now understand were *Historical and Social Perspectives: Advanced Theory, Practice and Research in*

Ecopsychology; The Experience of Place; and *Communication Across Cultures.*

Advanced Theory, Practice and Research in Ecopsychology was important to my progression as a student of ecopsychology because it helped me to understand that it truly is an integrated study. *Advanced Theory* also gave me a chance to build a foundation of knowledge regarding wilderness therapy. It was during my exploration of wilderness therapy research that I came across an article in which a group of adult women with varying backgrounds spent some time in the wilderness and walked away with "a sense of deep accomplishment...self-confidence and self-esteem" (Fredrickson & Anderson, 1999, p. 33). What struck me most about the article was that all the women seemed to liken their outdoor adventure to a spiritual experience. It is that natural world/spiritual experience connection that I carried with me into the *Communicating Across Cultures* class.

Communicating Across Cultures gave me the first chance to explore why and when transformation happens in the natural world. Inspired by my own Australian adventure and research that looked at "the wilderness experience as a source of spiritual inspiration," I chose the topic of pilgrimages to sacred sites in order to find what I was looking for (Fredrickson & Anderson, 1999, p. 38). It was not until I later studied spiritual development that I found *The Spiritual Brain: A Neuroscientist's Case for the*

Existence of the Soul by Mario Beauregard and Denyse O'Leary. Beauregard and O'Leary (2007) looked at spiritual experiences through the lens of neuroscience and found that moments of transformation were triggered by sacred places, depression or despair, prayer or meditation, and natural beauty (p. 199). This transformation did not change the character of the person, it changed their priorities which now included "a sense of purpose or new meaning to life and...a more compassionate attitude toward others" (p. 247).

The *Experience of Place* class not only gave me a chance to reflect on my own transformative experience in Australia, it introduced me to environmental historian Matthew Klingle. Klingle (2007) pointed out that the conservation movement and leisure activities in the 1930s created an awakening where "Americans now realized that in order to consume and enjoy nature, they needed to conserve and protect it" (p. 179). Between what Klingle wrote in *Emerald City: An Environmental History of Seattle* and what Fritz Hull put together in *Earth & Spirit: The Spiritual Dimension of the Environmental Crisis,* I was reminded that what we are struggling with in terms of the human/nature divide is not new. What I have since come to realize is that ecopsychology not only brings many ideas together, it helps give us permission to feel as we do, language to share our experiences, and tools to make a difference.

How has Ecopsychology Influenced This Project?

I chose to be creative with this project because I had previously worked on a documentary that wondered if "the good in man [had] expired" because we seemed to be "stealing all the love and the beauty from the land" (D. Rosalita, 2004). That documentary – *One Voice, One Love, One Spirit: A Sacred Gathering* – changed the way I viewed the human/nature relationship because it not only introduced me to the idea that we can negatively impact our environment, but that we should also care for Mother Earth as we care for ourselves.

With *Rooted in Water* as a book and video documentary I wanted to explore the importance of story in reconnecting people to the earth, and as a result, healing according to the principles of ecopsychology. What I learned from this project by focusing on the human/nature relationship is that our heritage is not just the land but the history of the use of the land and the impact of the current threat of overfishing. Our heritage is the care of the earth. Stories of Gullah Geechee losing their land rights have opened me up to the realization that this is not about ownership so much as it is about inheritance.

The passing down of land from one generation of Gullah Geechee to the next helps to demonstrate that caring for the land means caring for the survival of our children. Realizing that it is about the survival of our children has helped me to better understand the idea that "each generation should meet its needs without jeopardizing the prospects for future generations to meet their own needs" (Roszak, 1995, p. 75). Not only should we care for the land and consider it a part of our heritage, but that sense of stewardship should also be found in the idea of honoring ownership as a matter of inheritance...a matter of connecting generations...and a matter of lineage.

Summary/Discussion

Ecopsychology is the theoretical foundation of this project because it resonated with me and my experiences. I understand ecopsychology to be the study of the relationship of people and their environment with the recognition that they are part of an interrelated whole. I am attracted to the idea that part of that interrelated whole is nature, which is both alive and able to interact with me. The writers that excite me the most are those that speak to my idea of what ecopsychology could be, how the human/nature relationship could manifest itself, and how I could practice it so that I could help facilitate transformation.

Ecopsychology as a theoretical foundation has enabled me to explore my own relationship with the natural world as well as find a direction and a focus for my future work. My understanding of ecopsychology has been deepened by the stories of the Gullah Geechee because they have helped me to realize that the earth is part of our heritage and passing it on as an inheritance means that we can help care for our children and the generations that follow. One thing I would also add as a lesson from the Gullah Geechee is that we cannot simply hand over the land to our children without first communicating the value of that gift because a land this fertile "is where the gold is" (Appendix B). A lack of appreciation for the land and what it means to the family and the Gullah Geechee community is said to be why so much of it has been handed over to developers.

Where I think there is room to grow in terms of my theoretical foundation is in my understanding of phenomenology and transpersonal psychology. If phenomenology is about the ways in which we tell our story and transpersonal psychology gives us a more expansive means with which to view the human/nature relationship, then I think a deeper dive into those waters would also enrich and expand the way that I view ecopsychology.

In the end, I think that what I have learned as a result of my coursework has been just as impactful as the natural world encounters that have led me here. As a result of my explorations with this project I can see myself focusing on combining the elements of story, people, and place into a narrative ecopsychology practice. Such a practice, for me, would be the study of the human animal, its relationship to the environment, and how the two are connected and changed by story. By examining how story can help to make sense of, reveal, and even change the human/nature relationship, narrative ecopsychology as a practice, and ecopsychology in particular, can keep the voice of the earth as an intentional part of the conversation.

Chapter 4: Falling to Earth

Content, Methodology, and the Video Documentary

"Water is a way-finder in this world. Through receiving water's teaching, we can become more fluid and thus find appropriate responses to difficult problems. Water will dislodge us from where we are struck and set us afloat toward the fulfillment of our goals."

~ Malidoma Patrice Some

This chapter begins with an explanation of the process I used to craft the documentary *Rooted in Water: The Gullah Geechee People.* This creative part of the project focuses on the human/nature relationship of the descendents of enslaved Africans who are mindful about maintaining a connection to their ancestral heritage. For the purposes of this chapter quotes from the documentary material will not be cited, however the script I worked from to craft the documentary is located at Appendix B.

Methods and Procedures for Preparation

In preparation for collecting information for this application project I contacted Producer/Director Dominga Rosalita to see if she had any projects that related to the principles of ecopsychology as evidenced by an intentional relationship with the natural world. Rosalita was partial to what was then referred to as the *Sea Island Project* because it offered the most substance academically (D. Rosalita; personal communication; February 6, 2010). Rosalita and I corresponded about her research, literature review, proposal, and a video preview of the project. It was also recommended that I watch a feature entitled *Daughters of the Dust* as an example of the Gullah Geechee culture captured on video. I found the storyline of *Daughters of the Dust* difficult to follow and the audio, if not the language, difficult to understand. What I did recognize, like the ritual of wearing white outfits in a ceremonial situation, I had seen in previous video projects I crafted for Rosalita. As an additional way to prepare for this application project I used *Rooted in Water* as a focus for my assignments in the *Using Media for Social Change* class. Through those assignments I began to recognize the Gullah Geechee way of life as endangered. As an assignment I also interviewed Rosalita in order to find out what her intention was with the documentary. It is during this interview that I learned *Rooted in Water* was recorded during the summer of 2003 with the intention that there would be a return visit resulting in a three-part documentary series. As of this writing there has only been one visit resulting in 20 hours worth of footage. I also learned from my interview with Rosalita that the way the Gullah Geechee people pour libations, or drink offerings "poured out...to a deity" (Soanes, 2011), is unique and had never been capture on video before that summer.

Organizing, Analyzing, and Synthesizing Information/Data

In order to put together *Rooted in Water* as a documentary I began by transcribing the footage. Once I had an idea of how I wanted to incorporate the material in this book, I sent my proposal and a service agreement to Rosalita for consent (APPENDIX A) and finished transcribing the material. I organized the stories collected into a more concise script (APPENDIX B) and then proceeded to craft the documentary into a format that could be shown in a 90 minute symposium (APPENDIX C). The length of the documentary was also limited due to the fact that I was working with a VHS copy of the material because the original footage had been misplaced.

Constructing *Rooted in Water*

My usual practice in crafting a documentary is to transcribe all the materials that I have to work with and then organize everything in a way that both makes sense and tells a good story. What is different about *Rooted in Water* as a documentary is that I chose to include only the material that related to my coursework and the principles of ecopsychology. What is also different about how I crafted the documentary is that I established an outline for the content before I finished transcribing footage.

I Have a Dream

While transcribing the material for the documentary I came across a website that explained what made the *I Have a Dream* speech by Martin Luther King Junior brilliant. The flow between the idea of "what is," "what could be," and "the new bliss"

(Labarre, 2010) stood out for me as something that I wanted to follow for this project. In crafting a story with ecopsychology in mind, I did not just want to point out a problem or focus only on hope and promise. Instead I wanted to tell a story that could lead to action, understanding, and connection. Since this is a documentary involving the descendents of enslaved people, instead of 'what is,' 'what could be,' and 'the new bliss,' the documentary is segmented into "how it was," "how it is," and "how it shall be" both because it relates to the *Dream* speech themes and because this was the outline given by Marquetta "Queen Quet" Goodwine in talking about her vision for being able to be speak to others as a "[purveyor] of our story" and "[provider] of our culture" (Appendix B).

According to Suzanne Labarre (2010) in her analysis of the *Dream* speech, "what is" acknowledges what people are going through and could help others to identify or relate to the storyteller. As there are performances and stories from living historians about the slave trade, I have chosen to begin the documentary with "how it was" and then acknowledge what the descendents are dealing with in a section of "how it is." For Labarre "what could be" is a "call to action" or a "fulfillment of a promise that was made to us" (Labarre, 2010). I have reserved the call to action and references to "how it shall be" for the final section of the documentary so that I could both ensure a context and appreciation for how things shall be, as well as end with a positive message.

By exploring the elements of the *I Have a Dream* speech in how I crafted *Rooted in Water,* it was my hope to tell a story that reached inside of my audience, expanded the boundaries of what was known and spark in them an idea or an action that would ultimately help "to change the world" (Labarre, 2010) even if 'the world' in this case was the individual that received the story.

Using Media for Social Change

To establish the outline for *Rooted in Water* I also consulted the books used in my *Using Media for Social Change* class. Robert Bray, in his book titled *Spin Works!* (2000, 2002), includes a six step process for getting media attention for a story. It is in reviewing his suggestions that I am reminded that my goal here is to connect people to the natural world by providing a point of reference for them to identify why the land is sacred and how they might be able to honor that sacredness in a mindful way. The people I would ultimately be looking to reach are those who do feel disconnected from nature whether or not they realize it. The model that Bray suggests for sharpening my message is to define a problem, offer a solution that includes a message about my values, and finally a call to action that will help the person receiving the story get to the solution (p. 29). The problem, solution, call to action structure has three parts just as the 'what is,' 'what could be,' 'the new bliss' message of the *I Have a Dream* speech and the 'how it was,' 'how it is,' and 'how it will be' message of this version of the Gullah Geechee story. When I apply the Bray model to *Rooted in Water*, the problem is that the Gullah Geechee people are both losing their land and the connection to their heritage. The solution, as suggested by this documentary, is to know our true history, pass down what our elders have taught us, and maintain a connection to the land and our ancestors as an inheritance to our collective children. My intent with the organization and content of this documentary is to inspire people to either reach out to the Gullah Geechee Nation or to embrace their own story while recognizing that the environment is part of their heritage.

Discussion

The Gullah Geechee are a people of land and of water. Through representatives such as Queen Quet, they demonstrate a relationship to their natural environment by continuing to pump their own water; they work fields in cycles in order to give the land an appropriate amount of rest; and they fish the creek making sure to only take what is needed in the appropriate season to ensure the survival of the species.

For members of the Gullah Geechee Nation the connection to the past, to the water, and to each other is an intentional choice because they are contending with a population that has assimilated into mainstream culture and forgotten their language and skills. In order to encourage people to come back to the fold they want to let others know that they have to choose to practice what they know and they have to choose to share what they know in order to keep the culture alive.

The Gullah Geechee use the stories of 'how it was' when their ancestors were brought over on slave ships to illustrate the importance of water to their way of life. It is this understanding of history that Queen Quet says is missing from 'how it is' with developers who create gated communities and beach goers who do not appear to stop and reflect at the enormity of what had occurred on the water. This lack of recognition of 'how it was' could be at the center of a hurricane of implications that rise up and tear through 'how it shall be' in the future. In light of this journey I think story is not only a point of connection but a teacher of what is sacred.

Chapter 5: Back to the Lake

Content, Methodology, and the Beginning of a Practice in Narrative Ecopsychology

"Water is life. We are more water than anything else, just as Earth is mostly water."

~ Malidoma Patrice Some

In addition to *Rooted in Water: The Gullah Geechee People,* I was inspired to expand on my literature review by defining and outlining the foundation of a practice in narrative ecopsychology. This chapter not only establishes guidelines for the practice but, as an example, applies those guidelines to the raw material collected for the documentary. For the purposes of this chapter quotes pulled from the material will not be cited, however the script I used to craft the documentary is located at Appendix B.

Methods and Procedures for Preparation

In creating the foundation for narrative ecopsychology I began by searching the internet, Ohiolink database, and various book retailers for information on the study into the importance of story and found the subject of narratology. I then began searching 'narrative' in conjunction with 'ecopsychology' and 'psychology.' Based on my readings in narrative psychology I consider narrative ecopsychology to be the study of the impact of story on the human/nature relationship.

Many of the presentations, books, and articles I surveyed referred to story, and were aware of its use, but only one book put "story" and "ecopsychology" together in the title. *Out of the Shadow: Ecopsychology, Story, and Encounters with the Land* by

Rinda West (2007) views the field of ecopsychology as one that speaks for the land by challenging "anthropocentrism in ethics" (p. 192). West recognized that even the reading of a story "encourages a kind of introspective attention" that "allows the mind to connect the storied action with related experiences, so that what happens [in the story] can lead to insights about real problems" (p. 29). If enough people respond to a story, that story "can begin to reframe a culture's self-awareness" which leads to "a restoration through remembering" that is "crucial to our survival" (p. 194). But story, theory, or time in nature is "not enough to generate a new ethic" (p. 7). What is needed, according to West, is to give land access to a large number of people in addition to giving them "a new vision of the world that will reframe both our sense of ourselves and our ways of living with the land" (p. 7).

Inspired by *Out of the Shadows* I began a new search into the importance of story to ecopsychology. Using the quick search feature of Ohiolink, I selected nine different databases and searched "story ecopsychology," "narrative ecopsychology," "myth ecopsychology," and "case study ecopsychology." From those searches, the most relevant content was in the form of non-psychology journal articles that reviewed *Out of the Shadows*.

From a search of "story use in ecopsychology" of the internet, I found three websites. The one website that contained the most relevant, non-redundant content was *Ecopsychology: A Combination of Ecology, Psychology and Religion* by Tina Nussbaum (1998). In her paper, Nussbaum notes that "the first step to utilizing the principles of ecopsychology is to develop a relationship or understanding of the larger world," which involves "telling an ecological story as a starting point for a change in lifestyle" (p. 6). Under the topic of "Types of Ecotherapy," Nussbaum lists "reading a book, watching a video or any other environmental education resource" as options for ecopsychologists to raise ecological consciousness (p. 6). Following the lead of Nussbaum I found *Ecotherapy: Healing Ourselves, Healing the Earth* by Howard Clinebell (1996), which suggests that a "common creation story" (p. 95) will help facilitate change.

In going back to search "story ecotherapy" in 'all journals' and the nine different databases associated with Ohiolink, I found the same or similar results to the search for "story ecopsychology." In looking through Google Books I found *Nature-Guided Therapy* by George W. Burns (1998), which notes that folktales reveal "the importance of the environment" so that telling them in natural settings "allows for a person to identify and...access...memories" (p. 195). In *Everybody's Story*, Loyal Rue (2000) sees story as a way to "unite humanity" because the power of story "can do more than satisfy our longings to know, it also has the potential to arouse and direct the emotional regulators of behavior" (p. 132). Rue lists two of the three "moral concern" categories for story as "ecotherapy" and "psychotherapy" (p. 121). Ecotherapy, in this case, is a way to "foster the conditions for biospheric integrity," while psychotherapy is about "the imperative to act in ways that enhance the abilities of persons to achieve wholeness" (p. 121).

Through the Lens of Narrative Ecopsychology

I see the purpose of narrative ecopsychology as providing a larger context for the situation for which an individual is seeking meaning, but also in the creation of a planetary myth that offers a new vision for the world as Joseph Campbell and Rinda West have called for. This planetary myth would be a guiding story that gives "us a basis for expecting those separate threads" that help us to identify that our "wounds are so often intimately related to the wounds of the earth" (Ray & Anderson, 2000, p. 222). Just as story does not simply take a single form, the river of narrative should not either. I envision an expressive practice that, like the changing characteristics of water, can flow from art to music and craft to spoken or written word with the only requirement being that the narrative is mindful of the living system of earth and how people are part of that system. By allowing for an open and expressive element, narrative ecopsychology would also offer "creative and nontraditional writing and scholarship" just as the journal of *Ecopsychology* does with its designated Ecopsychology Narrative section (Doherty, 2009, p. 38).

The Molecules of the Narrative

As we step into the shallow waters of a practice in narrative ecopsychology, the three basic molecules that make up this application are story, people, and place. For me, the skillful weaving of the tales of the aboriginal people with the formation of the land by a tour guide is what inspired me to study ecopsychology. The molecules of story, people, and place were not properly bonded in my practicum experience however. Both while I was an apprentice on a wilderness quest and as a training field instructor for a wilderness therapy excursion, I craved to hear stories of both the earth and the native people, thinking it would have provided more of a context to the experience I was having. It is my point that by intentionally accounting for story, people, and place, the resulting meaning and context brought about by narrative ecopsychology could help to reveal the soul of the experience.

The story.

It is the story of slavery that ties the Gullah Geechee to Liverpool England where ships were built; to West Africa where 'black cargo' was loaded; to the southeast coast of the United States where they are rooted; and the waters in between. It is the story of the African genius that the Gullah Geechee people seek to reclaim when they reunite every year on Hilton Head to educate rather than entertain.

The people.

The Gullah Geechee are descendents of enslaved African and/or enslaved indigenous American people. For the most part they currently reside anywhere between North Carolina and Florida, maintain use of the Gullah language, the Geechee bridge language, spiritual practices, and other traditions that keep them connected to Africa and their ancestral heritage.

They are descendents of a people so genius that if you were to combine all the works of Africans from the Cooper River area in South Carolina, according to living historian Amil Jamal Terre, it would be "greater than the great work of the Pyramid of Egypt." Counted amongst the genius were skills in working with the trinity of "cotton, rice, and indigo" as well as an ability to "plot the sky with their naked eye." The Gullah Geechee are descendents of people that had "so much skill and ability," according to Queen Quet, "that that was why [they] were kidnapped in the first place."

The place.

The Gullah Geechee "are a people of land and a people of water." For them, water represents spirituality as well as being "about nurturing...healing...[and] a passage way." Ebo Landing is an example of water as a passage way because this is a place where many from the Ebo tribe were brought into the Sea Islands, taken to the auction blocks and then were believed to have walked back to Africa across the water in chains after refusing to be enslaved. In recognizing that water is part of their story, members of the Gullah Geechee nation do not gather without pouring libations as a tribute to their ancestors.

The Four Elements of the Narrative

In wading farther into the waters of a narrative ecopsychology practice, I think it appropriate to outline a basic structure for any event or ceremony not so much as an attempt to contain the experience but to ensure the voice of the earth is included. The introduction for *The Fifth Sacred Thing* by Starhawk gave me the structure for this practice by reminding me of the four elements of life: earth, air, fire, and water. In considering the elements in narrative ecopsychology, earth represents the story of the geological formation, systemic purpose, or creative metaphor of a place or land feature. Air, in this context, accounts for the story of the individual that is in search of meaning as well as the story of the native people. Fire represents the desire, passion, or purpose that is ignited by the experience. According to Clarissa Pinkola Estes (1992, 1995) passion is "not something to go 'get' but rather something generated in cycles and given out" (p. 142). The premise I am using here is the idea that what draws your attention while you are mindful and engaged in a sacred practice has meaning and indicates a direction to investigate or an action to take. Water, in a narrative ecopsychological practice, symbolizes both the mirroring that takes place as well as the act of reflecting on the experience.   By accounting for all the elements my intent is to tap into other sources of wisdom that might provide the resonance that help the person find the meaning they seek.

The protection of the earth.

The earth element of the *Rooted in Water* story recognizes that the Sea Islands of Georgia are barrier islands that "protect the mainland" to the extent that "if these islands are damaged or destroyed, eventually whatever happens here hits you." In fact the pollution of the island waterways has killed off seafood that feeds the people and the economy of the area as well as parts of the mainland.

The story is in the air.

Through the air I find that much of the land that was called home by the Gullah Geechee is in the hands of the developers or the State because people either did not know their property rights or were not aware of the value of the land. The land that the State has taken responsibility for is said to be demolished by neglect because "they're letting the chimneys our ancestors built...graves where their bodies are buried...be dilapidated." The land that has been taken over by developers has either been turned into gated communities or wildlife refuges. The Gullah Geechee who moved to the mainland of North Carolina did so because "they could no longer maintain control over their island cultures and communities." As a result of this move, some of the Gullah Geechee people have lost their language due to lack of use "because they had essentially been assimilated for survival purposes."

The passion for fire.

It is the continued loss of land that has inspired Queen Quet to educate people about their property rights. Being the "link to our ancestors" is why Elder Carlie Towne and Elder Halim Karim Gullahbemi created the Gullah Geechee Foundation. And it is in learning that the first people were from Africa that inspired a passion in Terre "to know who I am and who my people are...[and] the genius of Mother Africa that remains within us."

The reflection of water.

To maintain their connection the Gullah Geechee people begin their gatherings "with council of elders and pouring libations." In her 2003 reunion opening remarks Elder Towne pointed out the importance of taking care of community because "I am just a reflection of you" and through "sharing and networking...[their] efforts will provide a healing environment." For Queen Quet the healing environment is not only about learning our history, but also protecting "those things that we live in balance with."

The Seven Tasks of the Narrative

In still a deeper dive into what a practice in narrative ecopsychology could be, I was lead during a moment of reflection back to the work of Clarissa Pinkola Estes (1992, 1995) and "a series of seven tasks that teach one soul to love another deeply and well" (p. 145). These tasks suggest a structure for the cycles of the human/nature relationship.

Modified for the application of narrative ecopsychology the first task is the sudden discovery of the treasure of story, people, and place. This act of discovery will change the way the person regards the bonding of these molecules just as reflecting on my time in Australia changed the way that I view my relationship with nature. Next is the task of chasing and hiding which is the push/pull struggle a person goes through to deal with the treasure they have just found. Either simultaneously or in turns the person chases the meaning, the reasons for the discovery, and tries to hide from the implications. I imagine this to be much like the waves of fear and excitement I experienced when I woke up to the sound of galloping hooves at the end of my first wilderness quest solo fast. I feared being trampled but I was excited by the potential message carried by those hooves.

In the chasing and hiding from the treasure that was found some think that "they are running away from a relationship" but psychology, according to Pinkola Estes, would see this as a symptom of "the deeper issue of...misbelief and distrust" (p. 152). Those who run are said to fear living "according to the cycles of the wild and integral nature" (p. 152). It is also at this time that Pinkola Estes points out that "when the student is ready the teacher appears," bringing internal revelations for the soul (p. 153).

The third task is the untangling of the skeleton. In this case the person is examining the structure, the experience, and the meaning of the discovery. As an exploration of the elements of narrative ecopsychology, this task can include looking at the role of the natural environment in the discovery, the personal explanation of what happened and why, dealing with the strong emotions that surfaced as a result of the discovery, and what was revealed upon further reflection. This exploration leads to the task of resting and trusting in the presence of the discovery which is symbolized by sleep. With sleep it is implied that what was discovered will not cause harm nor will it disappear while the eyes are closed (p. 160).

The fifth task is a time of sharing and healing. At this point the person not only has some understanding of what he or she has found, but is able to communicate that discovery to others, and through that, a healing takes place as the drumming of the heart sings up new life. In this task the individual must both drum and sing. The drumming both represents and affects the heart while the singing offers gratitude and requests support from the community.

The final task of the narrative ecopsychology practice is the dance of the body and soul. Here the person physically moves their body, and through their body they move their soul (p. 145). With the movement of the soul, human and nature become one. As the story that inspired these tasks involved a harsh environment, stressed culture, and a requirement that a love relationship be a "visible bond" (p. 138) of endurance rather than a flight of fancy, I propose that these tasks also be our guides in the creation of a collective story as well as in the creation, maintenance, and development of the human/nature sustainable love relationship. The premise with these tasks is for the person to ultimately recognize the importance of the natural world and his or her relationship with it.

The sudden discovering the treasure of story, people, and place.

When it comes to *Rooted in Water,* the spiritual treasure is the story of the Gullah Geechee and what it means for our personal and collective history. In the case of prison inmates who were given information by Queen Quet regarding the history of the Gullah Geechee, some admitted that they "never knew our culture had all this history" and they began to feel as though they needed to educate other young men not to follow their path but to use their skills to "build a nation." According to Pinkola Estes, "in stories, as in life, the...quest [is begun] in one of three ways: in a sacred, or mean-spirited, or bumbling manner" (p. 146). In a journey through the story of Maurice and Cornelia Bailey, it was Cornelia who noted that many of their relatives began their quest in a bumbling manner because "it takes a while for black people to find themselves and recognize themselves as [Gullah Geechee]." This bumbling response means Cornelia "had to go in and pat them on the back and tell them who they are" until they are done "kicking and screaming and denying."

The task of chasing and hiding.

For the task of chasing and hiding I think of Carolee Brown who "had thrown…away" her skill of quilt making until she was asked by Queen Quet to bring back what she learned from her grandparents. Brown learned at a time when "neighbors and friends would get together and sit and sew," now Brown is the only one of six children that has picked up and passed on this treasure of tradition because her siblings were not interested in making quilts. Although her oldest daughter is too busy, the fact that her granddaughter has shown an interest in quilt making gives Brown hope that the tradition will continue.

The untangling the skeleton.

The task of untangling the meaning of the treasure and the "acceptance of the Life/Death/Life" (p. 152) cycle of a committed relationship could be akin to the untangling of the roots of the Gullah Geechee family tree. This Life/Death/Life cycle is not unlike a "living creature, obeying its own inner laws, [moving] through cycles of growth, [death], and…[rebirth] as a new creation" (Ray & Anderson, 2000, p. 264). In speaking of a commitment to move forward into the future, Queen Quet pointed out that as a foundation "we're the roots that hold up the tree" and if they "take care of the root they heal the tree." In the untangling a person progresses toward strengthening "one's ability to love" (p. 154) either their heritage if they are Gullah Geechee or the environment if the focus is on the human/nature relationship. Those who accomplish this will achieve "an enduring skill for love" (p. 154) which, in the case of ecopsychology, would be a sustainable human/nature relationship. Stepping into this task, the commitment to "touch the not-beautiful in another, and in ourselves" (p. 155) means going into the wild and being open to the response of nature because "without a task that challenges, there can be no transformation" (p. 154).

For the Gullah Geechee Nation untangling the meaning of what has been inherited could also be the process of answering the question what are you doing "to help the Nation?" The immediate answer, according to the elders, is for adults to take responsibility for themselves, for their children, and to hold each other accountable "for teaching our children about our history, about our African nation." For each person to be able to appreciate what it means to inherit the earth it also stands to reason that in the human/nature relationship adults must take responsibility for their part in the care of the earth as well as for what they teach the next generation in regards to the history of care and what it means to be a steward of the environment.

Resting and trusting in the presence of the discovery.

The relaxing into trust task, according to Pinkola Estes (1992, 1995), is symbolized by sleep but has to do with the belief that "any wound that comes...can be healed," that there will be a "new life," and that there is a "deeper meaning" (p. 163). Queen Quet trusts in the treasure of the Sea Islands and her ancestral heritage even as gated communities limit where she can now travel. When she is in the vicinity of the Atlantic Ocean, Queen Quet personally gives "thanks to the Creator...get[s] power from this energy...and then [pays] homage to all of my ancestors who are still in that space." Relaxing into trust of the human/nature relationship also means that we must believe that our wounds can be healed, that there will be new life and a deeper meaning, all of which makes it important to share our stories.

A time of sharing and healing.

At this point in the process, according to Pinkola Estes, a soul peers "into what the soul truly wants," admits the wound, and then weeps "for loss and love of both" (p. 164). For Queen Quet compassion comes when we are no longer simply concerned with recreation on the shores of the

Atlantic and become "grounded in all that they're walking over because there is so much blood...that I can hear...crying out from this soil." If we do not share the tear of compassion, Queen Quet believes that our ancestors are "going to rise up again and what other people recognize as a hurricane is going to wipe out a lot of what we see." This suggests that in order for our wounds to be healed we must show compassion for one another as well as for the land as it also cries. If we do not recognize the wounds in others, including in the earth, there will be consequences. As "only a hardness of heart inhibits weeping and union," Pinkola Estes points out that in some stories "tears change people, remind them of what is important, and save[s] their very souls" (Pinkola Estes, 1992, 1995, p. 167). Compassion not only recognizes the wounds of others, it acknowledges that we ourselves are wounded, and from that change happens.

The drum of the heart sings up new life.

The enslaved Africans had drums that allowed them to communicate at the rate of 100 miles per hour. When the drums were taken away they used their hands "to raise the spirits." In recognizing that "the heartbeat is our first drum" the Gullah Geechee gather, "let the drums resound" and "make their way to where the Africans went." According to Pinkola

Estes "it is the heart that enables us to love as a child loves" and the "singing of sound and using the heart" as a drum that serves as "acts awakening layers of the psyche not much used or seen" (p. 169). As a living historian Terre sees his role as trying "to get some of the eyes to open up where they're no longer blind, where they no longer have the hard heart." If it is our heart that opens us to child-like wonder and the expressing of our heart so that it beats like a drum that awakens us, then it is the sharing of stories by our living historians that will prepare our hearts and us for new life.

The dance of body and soul.

The dance of the Gullah Geechee is the shout. The shout "comes out of a movement that...[is] counterclockwise" because it is tied to the hajj, or the required Muslim pilgrimage to Mecca. Although some Africans later became Christians because of the incorporation of water in celebrations, the shout is traced to the African Muslims who could no longer make the trek to Mecca after they were brought to the United States. Queen Quet sees the shout as coming out of spaces that are "painful to have to touch" but which demonstrated that "your ancestors had to be strong to endure and still be able to create the spirituals." As the physical movement of the body opens the soul to a union with nature, dance as a task is an expression, a release of pain.

Discussion

By defining and establishing guidelines for a practice in narrative ecopsychology I have attempted to create a process with which to look at the development of the human/nature relationship and how it can be sustainable "during various still-water times" (Pinkola Estes, 1992, 1995, p. 173). By wading into the process at increasingly deeper levels I look to honor the idea of meeting people where they are and allowing them to ease into an awareness that will call forth their next teacher. Once that awareness is achieved, "it is your soul's work to not overlook what has been brought up, to recognize treasure as treasure no matter how unusual its form, and to consider carefully what to do next" (p. 146).

By using the story captured by the creation of a video documentary as an example with which to apply the guidelines of narrative ecopsychology, I tested my ideas to see if additional insights could be brought to the surface. If I had the guidelines for narrative ecopsychology during the beginning of my studies I believe it would have been easier for me to convey to Producer/Director Dominga Rosalita what I was looking for from the material for this project.

All the rest aside, the development of guidelines for a practice in narrative ecopsychology is a response to the new vision, the new story that is to reframe who we are as people and our relationship with nature. In the shallow end of the narrative ecopsychology pool were the molecules of story, people, and place. This structure was meant to give context and soul to an experience and helped me to recognize that the story of water in their bloodline is what connects the Gullah Geechee to the planet, the genius of their ancestors gives the Gullah Geechee a legacy of skills to draw from, and the determination of one tribe lets the Gullah Geechee know that they can fly.

Wading deeper into the pool of narrative ecopsychology I found that the Sea Islands as barrier islands could be seen as a metaphor for the Gullah Geechee people. If we do not protect their way of life, whatever happens to them could happen to us. A look at property rights, creating a healing environment, and the importance of understanding your lineage are multiple stories that could speak to unrecognized value. That unrecognized value is what we are contending with in regards to the human/nature relationship as well.

In the deepest waters of narrative ecopsychology I found a new level of intimacy with the Gullah Geechee that I believe could speak to society as a whole. How a person struggles to accept, embrace, and celebrate the realization that they are descendants of an enslaved people can mirror how people choose to commit to a sustainable human/nature relationship. What I appreciate about the tasks of developing a love relationship with nature is that there is a task that includes full body immersion through drumming, dancing, and singing. Just as we know water "by letting it wash over us" (Chalquist, 2009, p. 255), the immersion in a full body experience is important in the human/nature relationship because it forces us to face our fear of wildness and submerge ourselves in "an unceasing invitation to drop our defenses and once more flow with the cycles of the natural world" (Chalquist, 2009, p. 254).

Chapter 6: Seeping Through as Inspiration

Summary and Discussion

"Water cannot be limited or owned; its will is to be free. Water searches for ways to fit in, to align with ambient conditions, and to bring vitality to nature and the Earth."

~ Malidoma Patrice Some

With this book I wanted to know if story could connect people to a place. If it could, knowledge of that and intentionally including story in the facilitation of that connection meant bringing people to wholeness through the principles of ecopsychology. While building a foundation for my own understanding of the importance of story, I chose to apply what I learned to the story of the Gullah Geechee people. Just as "we can look to water as an indicator of the health of the planet" (Some, 2009, p. 253) we can look to the Gullah Geechee as an indicator of the health of our own environmental heritage. Land that was no longer able to stay in their family has been developed for recreation, reserved for wildlife, or set aside for future generations but neglected.

Summary

Through this project I was able to establish that stories in any form could connect people to the natural world depending on the appropriateness of the story, the authenticity of the teller, and the openness of the person receiving the story. Stories are a means of participating because they allow us to find meaning in our experiences. Stories can also be seen as part of the solution in the "problem...solution...call to action" model of messaging (Bray, 2000, 2002, p. 29). In fact ecological stories are seen as the first step to developing the human/nature relationship in ecotherapy because they raise consciousness which leads to a "change in lifestyle" (Nussbaum, 1998, p. 6).

For the Gullah Geechee, stories of their heritage ensure that the next generation knows "who they are even in the midst of the concrete jungle." This realization expanded my understanding of heritage to include a connection between generations as well as a deeper appreciation for the need to take care of the earth so that our children understand the value of what they inherit. Personally, I reconsidered what it would mean to inherit property from my parents and that has inspired me to not only build a foundation for my children, but to make sure that they understand the value of what I am offering. The other thing I take away from the Gullah Geechee story is a need to have elders give context to 'how it is' with stories of 'how it was.'

Inspired by my literature review and the need for a new vision or story with which to frame the human/nature relationship and facilitate change, this book evolved to include the beginning of a practice in narrative ecopsychology. With this practice my goal is to have a new focus for storytelling that is not intended to put me in the role of "fortune-teller" so much as "a deep-sea diver, plunging beneath the obvious appearances to see the possible alternatives and their implications" (Ray & Anderson, 2000, p. 237).

I see the journey of a narrative ecopsychology practice as following the "world as lover" path that

Joanna Macy (1991) laid out (p. vii). Because "love requires understanding" the relationship tasks from a practice in narrative ecopsychology would help "us understand how we can heal this interconnected, interpenetrating universe" (p. vii). Another benefit to the tasks of narrative ecopsychology is that they teach one to love another "just as lovers seek for union, we are apt, when we fall in love with our world, to fall into oneness with it as well" (Macy, 1991, p. 11).

Possible Future Projects for Me

Upon completing this project I began a year-long reflection on and evaluation of the guidelines I laid out for the practice of narrative ecopsychology. My intent was to continue to train as a guide for quests but also to facilitate natural world experiences that permit me to witness, collect, and share stories. What I learn from this time of reflection and experience will be collected and shared in a book as well as a blog (NarrativeEcopsych.Wordpress.com) that will also operate as a searchable database. Among the work that will feed that database is a deeper survey of literature that should include works from Theodore Sarbin regarding narrative psychology, works categorized as ecocriticism, as well as more specifically *Nature, Earthdance,* and *The Universe Story.*

Possible Future Projects for the Ecopsychological Community.

James Hillman and Michael Ventura (1993) have already pointed out that the world was getting worse after 100 years of psychotherapy. If ecopsychology is a response to a world that was getting worse, then narrative ecopsychology could be a reminder that after nearly 20 years of intentionally giving voice to the earth we are still in need of a common planetary myth or new vision for the world. This new vision must reach from the expanse of the cosmic evolution of the universe into the intimate depths of the human/nature relationship. While *The Universe Story* is a "narrative of our own developmental journey through time and space" (Macy, 1991, p. 83), I propose the common story that is to be our new vision includes a collection of personal accounts from many cultures which could be an application of the research being done by the HINTS Lab at the University of Washington. By incorporating the use of personal stories we are recognizing them as "maps of some of the major land-marks and compass settings for the journey" that transitions those who are disconnected from nature back into a connection. In the end the new vision that re-imagines the human/nature relationship should be like a museum in the Gullah Geechee community where it is the story of the people that determines the meaning of the museum rather than having the museum tell "you what your story is."

In the interest of developing a story that reframes the human/nature relationship, one future project could be a narrative ecopsychology class looking at the importance and use of story in ecopsychology. Pending other publications, required reading could be *The Power of Myth*; *Women Who Run with the Wolves*; *Out of the Shadow;* and *Ecotherapy: Healing Ourselves, Healing the Earth* which proved to be helpful and relevant to my literature exploration. The narrative ecopsychology class can later be expanded into a program that begins with a look at the importance of story after an introduction to ecopsychology. The foundation of the program should also include a look at narrative psychology for a baseline of understanding, phenomenology for documentation, as well as a look at the use of story in ecotherapy practices.

Another future project for the field of ecopsychology could be an anthology compiling explorations and reflections on the use of story in the field by first and second generation ecopsychologists. Specifically among the contributors could be Jan Edl Stein and her use of story to open patients up to the natural world as indicated by her part of the

Ecopsychology Emerging presentation at the Bioneers conference in October 2010. As the anthology emerges, there could be a narrative journal created that services an interdisciplinary community as a means to not just "build bridges across areas of research that have been separated" but to "weave connections between people in different professions" (Ray & Anderson, 2000, p. 195). Weaving connections between people is beautifully illustrated by Paul Hawken in *Blessed Unrest* where the work of Ralph Waldo Emerson is linked to Henry David Thoreau, whose work is linked to Mahatma Gandhi, whose work is linked to Martin Luther King Junior (pp. 74, 79, 84). In advance of an interdisciplinary journal focused on the importance of story, there could be a special edition of the *Ecopsychology* journal dedicated to the use of story in the field.

I suggest that if ecocriticism is the main category for this work then story explorations involving the environment be sub-categorized as narrative ecopsychology because "a critical aspect of telling the new stories is calling things by their true names" (Ray & Anderson, 2000, p. 223). By creating a sub-category which could serve as a bridge to the field of ecopsychology, it is my point that an examination of the impact of story on the human/nature relationship is not just about being critical. While ecocritical literature may look at the "relationships between things,...human culture, and the physical world" (Glotfelty & Fromm, 1996, p. xx), it does so with the intent to examine how the "metaphors of nature and land are used and abused" (Glotfelty & Fromm, 1996, p. 81). I am proposing that a sub-category of narrative ecopsychology be the exploration and study of maintaining, developing, or reviving the human/nature relationship through an experiential understanding.

In the interest of sharing knowledge so that future generations may benefit, I also propose the creation of a database where dissertations are at least informally published and made available to students, graduates, and professionals in any country. The reason I am emphasizing the compilation and sharing of information is not just because I now consider it a part of our heritage, but because the common knowledge of the use of story and the benefits of ecocritical works were not apparent during my own research. I think by providing easier access to information and a basic understanding of how that information relates to any given field first and second generation ecopsychologists will be empowered to "train your replacements before you go" so that future ecohealers "don't...get dependent on you" (Starhawk, 1993, p. 196) to fill in the blanks. Wherever this journey leads in the future, I do know that this is the beginning of a deeper personal understanding of how we each can begin to heal the world – and ourselves – one story at a time.

Discussion

What this project implies for the field of ecopsychology is the importance of publishing work and passing along an understanding that would allow future generations to take root in a solid foundation of ideas that they can share, evolve, and carry from the past into the future. After all, like the nation the Gullah Geechee, we must teach the next generation the value of their heritage because "if we don't teach them how to fight and hold on, it will sure enough be gone."

The strength of this project is in recognizing the importance of story to ecopsychology as a resource with which to bring people into their own awareness. Where this project can be expanded is in the inclusion of additional literature as is evidenced by my suggestion for future projects. If I knew in the beginning what I now understand I would have concentrated on establishing guidelines for narrative ecopsychology and applied them to multiple stories with the intent of examining change in the human/nature relationship.

The difficult part of putting this project together was the seemingly endless amount of time that it took to prepare to edit the documentary. My focus on the importance of story on the human/nature relationship meant that I could immediately recognize what material would not be included in the final video; however it was still a large time commitment to transcribe the material. After I transcribed the raw material it took a few days for me to organize everything into the script that is featured in Appendix B. After I had the script I immediately realized that it would take a lot of time to go back and forth on VHS tapes. As a result I then organized each sound bite referenced by the script in ascending order so that I could record everything I would need into the computer more efficiently.

It took another week to not only get all the video into the computer but to make sure that I had enough space on the computer to accommodate the material. Once I had all the material in the computer, the easy access of footage allowed for both a quick editing process as well as freedom to experiment with the weaving of the story. Much of what I had scripted (Appendix B) was left out so that I could play the finished product (Appendix C) in its entirety during my symposium.

Reflection

Just as nothing is wasted in the sustainable cycle of water, nothing of who I used to be was wasted in the creation of this application project. I was a video storyteller that had memorable outdoor experiences while in search of the next wave of purpose for my life. I emerged from this pool of experience with a lifetime worth of work to do, a heart full of appreciation, and a rooting in ecopsychology.

I have equated story with water. Through this application project I have recognized that with the chance to wash away boundaries of who we are and who we can be as part of a living system, there is a power and importance in also being rooted in story. Because stories nurture our connection to the rest of the living system it is important to be mindful of their power to teach, their power to reveal, and their power to heal. If we recognize that it is not about using story so much as it is about respecting story as an elder, then the tide of tales will be a continuous cycle of wisdom for generations to come.

Chapter 7: Emptying in to the Ocean
References and Bibliography

"When we try to control water's desire to reconnect with itself, we disrupt its capacity to satisfy the thirst of the human community."

~ Malidoma Patrice Some

References

Adichie, C. (Performer). (2009, July). *The danger of the single story.* United States of America. http://www.ted.com/talks/lang/eng/chimamanda_adichie_the_danger_of_a_single_story.html

Aizenstat, S. (1995). Jungian psychology and the world unconscious. In T. Roszak, M. E. Gomes, & A. D. Kanner (Eds.), *Ecopsychology: Restoring the earth, healing the mind* (pp. 92-100). San Francisco, CA: Sierra Club Books.

Beauregard, M., & O'Leary, D. (2007). *The spiritual brain: A neuroscientist's case for the existence of the soul.* New York, NY: Harper One.

Booknews.com. (1997-2010). *Voice of the earth.* Retrieved January 18, 2010, from Barnesandnoble.com: http://search.barnesandnoble.com/Voice-of-the-Earth/Theodore-Roszak/e/9781890482800/?itm=8&USRI=theodore+roszak

Bray, R. (2000, 2002). *Spin works! A media guidebook for communicating values and shaping opinion.* San Francisco, CA: Independent Media Institute.

Brody, H. (2000). *The other side of eden: Hunters, farmers, and the shaping of the world.* New York City, NY: North Point Press.

Brown, B. (Performer). (2010, June). *The power of vulnerability.* Houston, TX. Available from http://www.ted.com/talks/lang/eng/brene_bro wn_on_vulnerability.html

Brown, L. R. (1995). Ecopsychology and the environmental revolution. In T. Roszak, M. E. Gomes, & A. D. Kanner (Eds.), *Ecopsychology; restoring the earth, healing the mind.* San Francisco, CA: Sierra Club Books.

Burns, G. W. (1998). *Nature-guided therapy: Brief integrative strategies for health and well-being.* Philadelphia, PA: Brunner/Mazel.

Ecotherapy: Healing with nature in mind. (2009). (L. Buzzell, & C. Chalquist, Trans.) San Francisco, CA: Sierra Club Books.

Cahalan, W. (1995). Ecological groundedness in gestalt theory. In T. Roszak, M. E. Gomes, & A. D. Kanner (Eds.), *Ecopsychology: Restoring the earth, healing the mind* (pp. 216-223). San Francisco, CA: Sierra Club Books.

Campbell, J., & Moyers, B. D. (1988). *The power of myth.* (B. S. Flowers, Ed.) Anchor Books.

Chalquist, C. (2009). A look at the ecotherapy research evidence. *Ecopsychology* , *1* (2).

Chalquist, C. (2009). Commentary by Craig Chalquist. In L. Buzzell, & C. Chalquist (Eds.), *Ecotherapy: Healing with nature in mind* (pp. 253-255). San Francisco, CA: Sierra Club Books.

Clayton, S., & Myers, G. (2009). *Conservation psychology: Understanding and promoting human care for nature.* Hoboken, NJ: Wiley-Blackwell.

Clinebell, H. (1996). *Ecotherapy: Healing ourselves, healing the earth.* Minneapolis, MN: Augsburg Fortress.

Cohen, M. J. (2000, August). *Nature connected psychology: creating moments that let earth teach.* (M. Press, Editor, & International Community of Ecopsychology) Retrieved November 10, 2009, from Gatherings: seeking ecopsychology: http://www.ecopsychology.org/journal/gatherings3/cohen.html

Davis, C. S. (December 2006). Sylvia's story: Narrative, storytelling, and power in a children's community mental health system of care. *Qualitative Inquiry* , *12* (6), 1220-1243.

Davis, W. (Performer). (2003, February). *Endangered cultures.* Long Beach, CA. Available from:

http://www.ted.com/talks/lang/eng/wade_dav is_on_endangered_cultures.html

Doherty, T. J. (Ed.). (2009). Ecopsychology narrative. *Ecopsycholgy , 1* (1), 38-46.

Dossey, L. M. (2009). The power of story: Observations from a book tour. *Explore , 5* (6), 309-312.

Drengson, A., & Devall, B. (Eds.). (2008). *The ecology of wisdom: The writings of Arne Naess.* Berkeley, CA: Counterpoint Press.

Ferguson, G. (2009). *Shouting at the sky: Troubled teens and the promise of the wild* (Paperback ed.). New York, NY: Sweetgrass Books.

Fisher, A. (2009). Ecopsychology as Radical Praxis. In L. Buzzell, & C. Chalquist (Eds.), *Ecotherapy; healing with nature in mind* (pp. 60-68). San Francisco, CA: Sierra Club Books.

Fisher, A. (2002). *Radical ecopsychology: Psychology in the service of life.* Albany, NY: State University of New York Press.

Fredrickson, L. M., & Anderson, D. H. (1999). A qualitative exploration of the wilderness experience as a source of spiritual inspiration. *Journal of Environmental Psychology , 19* (1), 21-39.

Glotfelty, C., & Fromm, H. (Eds.). (1996). *The ecocriticism reader: Landmarks in literary ecology.* Athens, GA: University of Georgia Press.

Greenway, R. (2009). The wilderness experience as therapy: We've been here before. In L. Buzzell, & C. Chalquist (Eds.), *Ecotherapy; healing with nature in mind* (pp. 132-139). San Francisco, CA: Sierra Club Books.

Harper, S. (1995). *The way of the wilderness* (Vols. Ecopsychology; restoring the earth, healing the mind). (T. Roszak, M. E. Gomes, & A. D. Kanner, Eds.) San Francisco, CA: Sierra Club Books.

Hawken, P. (2007). *Blessed unrest: How the largest movement in the world came into being and why no one saw it coming.* London, England: Viking Penguin.

Johnson, C. Y. (1998). A consideration of collective memory in African American attachment to wildland recreation places. *Research in Human Ecology , 5* (1), 5-15.

Kahn, J. P., Severson, R. L., & Rockert, J. H. (2009). The human relation with nature and technological nature. *Association for Psychological Science , 18* (1), 37-42.

Kapur, S. (Performer). (2009, November). *We are the stories we tell ourselves.* Mysore, India. http://www.ted.com/talks/lang/eng/shekhar_k

apur_we_are_the_stories_we_tell_ourselves.ht
ml

Kelly, S. (1993). The path of place. In F. Hull (Ed.), *Earth and spirit; the spiritual dimension of the environmental crisis* (pp. 105-113). New York, NY: The Continuum Publishing Company.

Kim, U., & Park, Y.-S. (2006). The scientific foundation of indigenous ad cultural psychology; The transactional approach. In U. Kim, K.-S. Yang, & K.-K. Hwang (Eds.), *Indigenous and cultural psychology: Understanding people in context* (pp. 27-). New York, NY: Spring Science+Business Media, LLC.

Klein, J. (Performer). (2010, February). *Photos that changed the world.* Long Beach, CA. http://www.ted.com/talks/lang/eng/jonathan_klein_photos_that_changed_the_world.html

Klingle, M. (2007). *Emerald city: An environmental history of Seattle.* New Haven & London: Yale University Press.

Kumar, S., Deravy, E., & Kumar Mitchell, M. (2009). *Earth pilgrim.* Foxholle, Dartington, Totnes, Devon, UK: Green Books Ltd.

Labarre, S. (2010). *Infographic: What makes MLK's "I have a dream" speech brilliant.* (Mansuueto Ventures, LLC) Retrieved February 17, 2011, from Fastgodesign.com:

http://www.fastcodesign.com/1663103/infogra
phic-what-makes-mlks-i-have-a-dream-speech-
brilliant

LaDuke, W. (2006). Foreword. In C. Schaefer,
*Grandmothers counsel the world; Women
elders offer their vision for our planet* (pp. xi-
xii). Boston, MA: Trumpeter Books.

Liebert, E. (2000). *Changing life patterns: Adult
development in spiritual direction* (Expanded
ed.). Danvers, MA: Copyright Clearance Center.

Liebert, R. M., & Liebert, L. L. (1998). *Personality:
Strategies and issues* (8th ed.). Pacific Grove,
CA: Brooks/Cole Publishing Company.

Maathai, W. (2010). *Replenishing the earth: Spiritual
values for healing ourselves and.* New York, NY:
Random House, Inc.

Mack, J. E. (1995). The politics of species arrogance. In
T. Roszak, M. E. Gomes, & A. D. Kanner (Eds.),
*Ecopsychology: Restoring the earth, healing the
mind* (pp. 279-287). San Francisco, CA: Sierra
Club Books.

Macy, J. (1991). *World as lover, world as self: Courage
for global justice and ecological renewal.*
Berkeley, CA: Parallax Press.

Macy, J., & Young Brown, M. (1998). *Coming back to
life: Practices to reconnect our lives, our world.*
Gabriola Island, BC, Canada: New Society
Publishers.

Meadows, D. H. (2008). *Thinking in systems: A primer.* White River Junction, VT: Chelsea Green Publishing Company.

Moon, J., & Fowler, J. (2008). 'There is a story to be told...': A framework for the conception of story in higher education and professional development. *Nurse Education Today* , 232-239.

Newman, P., & Jennings, I. (2008). *Cities as sustainable ecosystems: Principles and practices.* Washington, D.C.: Island Press.

Nussbaum, T. (1998, November 23). *Ecopsychology: A combination of ecology, psychology, and religion.* Retrieved January 15, 2011, from Goshen.edu: http://www.goshen.edu/bio/Biol410/BSSPapers98/nussbaum.html

Rosalita, D. (Producer). (2004). *One voice, one love, one spirit: A sacred gathering* [Motion Picture]. Philadelphia, PA.

Oxford University Press. (2011). *Dictionary.* Retrieved March 11, 2011, from Oxford Dictionaries: http://oxforddictionaries.com/

Pattanaik, D. (Performer). (2009, November). *East versus West: The myths that mystify.* Mysore, India. Available at:

http://www.ted.com/talks/lang/eng/devdutt_p
attanaik.html

Pinkola Estes, C. P. (1992, 1995). *Women who run with
the wolves: Myths and stories of the wild
woman archetype.* New York, NY: Ballantine
Books.

Plotkin, B. (2003). *Soulcraft: Crossing into the mysteries
of nature and psyche.* Novato, CA: New World
Library.

Poulos, C. N. (February 2006). The ties that bind us, the
shadows that separate us: Life and death,
shadow and (dream) story. *Qualitative Inquiry ,
12* (1), 96-117.

Poulos, C. N. (February 2006). The ties that bind us, the
shadows that separate us; Life and death,
shadow and (dream) story. *Qualitative Inquiry ,
12* (1), 96-117.

Ray, P. H., & Anderson, S. R. (2000). *The cultural
creatives: How 50 million people are changing
the world.* New York, NY: Harmony Books.

Redfield, J. (1997). The tenth insight: Holding the
vision. In J. Redfield, *The celestine insights* (pp.
1-236). New York, NY: Warner Books, Inc.

Romano McGraw, P. (2007). *Seeking the wisdom of the
heart: Reflections on seven stages of spiritual
development.* Wilmette, IL: Baha'i Publishing.

Rosalita, D. (Producer). (2003). *Rooted in water: The Gullah Geechee people* [Motion Picture]. Pittsburgh, PA.

Roszak, T. (1992, 2001). *The voice of the earth; An exploration of ecopsychology* (2nd ed.). Grand Rapids, MI: Phanes Press, Inc.

Roszak, T. (1995). Where psyche meets gaia. In T. G. Roszak, *Ecopsychology, restoring the earth healing the mind* (p. 5). San Francisco: Sierra Club Books.

Roszak, T. (1998). *Ecopsychology: Eight principles.* Retrieved January 11, 2010, from Ecopsychology on-line: Introducing ecopsychology: http://ecopsychology.athabascau.ca/Final/intro.htm

Rue, L. (2000). *Everybody's story: Wising up to the epic of evolution.* Albany, NY: State University of New York Press.

Sams, J., & Carson, D. (1988). *Medicine cards; the discovery of power through the ways of animals.* San Fe, NM: Bear & Company.

Schaefer, C. (2006). *Grandmothers counsel the world.* Boston, MA: Trumpeter Books.

Shepard, P. (1995). Nature and madness. In T. G. Roszak, *Ecopsychology, restoring the earth healing the mind.* (p. 34). San Francisco: Sierra Club Books.

Sierpina, V. S., Kreitzer, M. J., Mackenzie, E. P., & Sierpina, M. P. (2007). Regaining our humanity through story. *Explore , 3* (6), 626-632.

Soanes, C. (Ed.). (2011). *Oxford dictionaries definition.* (Oxford University Press) Retrieved April 07, 2011, from Oxford dictionaries online: http://oxforddictionaries.com/

Some, M. P. (2009). A shamanic reflection on water. In L. Buzzell, & C. Chalquist (Eds.), *Ecotherapy: Healing with nature in mind* (pp. 251-255). San Francisco, CA: Sierra Club Books.

Starhawk. (1993). *The fifth sacred thing.* New York, NY: Bantom Books

Stewart, E. C., & Bennett, M. J. (1991). *American cultural patterns: A cross-cultural perspective* (Revised ed.). Yarmouth, ME: Intercultural Press, Inc.

Ward, D. (2003). *The water cycle: Water on the move.* (The National Center for Atmospheric Research & the UCAR Office of Programs) Retrieved January 11, 2011, from Weather & climate basics: http://www.eo.ucar.edu/basics/wx_1_c.html

West, R. (2007). *Out of the shadow: Ecopsychology, story, and encounters with the land.* Charlottesville, VA: University of Virginia Press.

Rooted In Water

Bibliography

Beach, L. R. (2010). *The psychology of narrative thought: How the stories we tell ourselves shape our lives.* Bloomington, IN: Xlibris Corporation.

Bettmann, J. E., & Jasperson, R. A. (2007). Adults in wilderness treatment: A unique application of attachment theory and research. *Clinical Social Work Journal , 36* (1), 51-61.

Bruner, J. (2004). Life as narrative. *Social Research , 71* (3), 691-710.

Cohen, M. J. (2000, August). *Nature connected psychology: creating moments that let earth teach.* (M. Press, Editor, & International Community of Ecopsychology) Retrieved November 10, 2009, from Gatherings: seeking ecopsychology: http://www.ecopsychology.org/journal/gatherings3/cohen.html

Davis, J. P. (2003, Spring). *Overview of Transpersonal Psychology.* Retrieved November 2, 2010, from John V. Davis: http://www.johnvdavis.com/tp/overviewTP.htm

Guber, P. (2011). *Tell to win: Connect, persuade, and triumph with the hidden power of story.* New York, NY: Crown Business.

Laszlo, J. (2008). *An introduction to narrative psychology.* New York, NY: Psychology Press.

Laszlo, J. (2008). *The science of stories: An introduction to narrative psychology.* New York, NY: Psychology Press.

Meeker, J. W. (1993). Practical environmental mythology. In F. Hull (Ed.), *Earth and spirit: The spiritual dimension of the environmental crisis* (pp. 150-155). New York, NY: The Continuum Publishing Company.

Mortola, P., & Carlson, J. (2003). "Collecting an anecdote": The role of narrative in school consultation. *The Family Journal: Counseling and Therapy for Couples and Families , 11* (1), 7-12.

Norton, C. L. (2009). Ecopsychology and social work: Creating an interdisciplinary framework for redefining person-in-environment. *Ecopsychology , 1* (3), 138-.

Olsen, B. (2004). *Sacred places around the world: 108 destinations* (2nd ed.). San Francisco, CA: Consortium of Collective Consciousness.

Rosalita, D. (Producer). (2004). *One voice, one love, one spirit: A sacred gathering* [Motion Picture]. Philadelphia, PA.

Rosalita, D. (Producer). (2003). *Rooted in water: The Gullah/Geechee people* [Motion Picture]. Pittsburgh, PA.

Scheibe, K. E. (April 2006). Theodore R. Sarbin (1911-2005). *American Psychologist , 61* (3), 249-250.

Watkins, M. (2009). Creating restorative ecotherapeutic practices. In L. Buzzell, & C. Chalquist (Eds.), *Ecotherapy; healing with nature in mind* (pp. 219-236). San Francisco, CA: Sierra Club Books.

Chapter 8: Vapor Warmed by the Sun

Appendix

"Water is not just a resource. It is a living being with much to teach us about patience, fluidity, and adaptability."

~ Craig Chalquist

Appendix A: Service Agreement

SERVICE AGREEMENT:
VIDEO EDITING AND PRODUCTION

This Agreement is entered into on this first day of February, 2011, by and between Totally Divine Video Editing ("Totally Divine"), a Washington Limited Liability Company, and Dominga Rosalita and Sisebon Productions ("Sisebon").

In consideration of the mutual promises set forth hereunder, the sufficiency of which is hereby acknowledged, Totally Divine and Sisebon agree to the following:

1.   Totally Divine agrees to provide story/video editing services to Sisebon. Specific information on the project is attached to this Agreement and shall be incorporated by reference herein. The parties agree that Tiffany A. Dedeaux will receive "Story Editor" and "Video Editor" titles in the credits. The project includes #5 copies on DVD.

2.   Totally Divine agrees to provide for the project, Totally Divine irrevocably grants to Dominga Rosalita the right, in perpetuity, throughout the world, in all media, now or hereafter known, to use the edited version of a documentary entitled *Rooted in Water: The Gullah/Geechee People* in any manner she deems appropriate, without limitation, by whatever means exhibited, advertised or exploited.

3.   Dominga Rosalita agrees to pay Totally Divine 50 per for its services in lieu of granting Tiffany Dedeaux full editorial judgment over how and what to include in the project. In addition Tiffany is granted permission to use *Rooted in Water* and its materials for a student application project at Antioch University Seattle.

4.   Totally Divine is not responsible for acquiring permission to use any materials in the project that are included by Dominga Rosalita, Sisebon, or any participants in the materials for *Rooted in Water*.

5.   Totally Divine agrees that no parts of this project may be used in any public or private screenings that is not associated with the student application project without the express written consent of Dominga Rosalita. Totally Divine shall keep a copy of the project to use in the promotion of its services and reserves the right to submit the project for awards and show prospective employers or clients a work sample including cuts from this work. Totally Divine is also permitted to use Freeze Frames of the project to post on its website and to stream segments of this documentary over the Internet. Totally Divine retains no additional present or future rights to *Rooted in Water* other than those enumerated in this agreement.

6.   Totally Divine shall retain intellectual property rights in its work in connection with the project subject to Sisebon's license for use as set out above.

7.   Time shall be of the essence in the performance of this Agreement.

8.   The failure of either party to insist in any one or more instances upon performance of any terms or conditions of this Agreement shall not be construed a waiver of future performance of any such term, covenant or condition but the obligations of either party with respect thereto shall continue in full force and effect.

9.   If any part of this Agreement is held unenforceable for any reason, the remaining portion of this Agreement shall remain in full force and effect, and shall be carried out in a manner, which is consistent with the intentions of the parties hereto.

10.   Either party may terminate this Agreement upon thirty (30) days written notice to the other. In the event of termination by Sisebon, Totally Divine returns the edited materials completed to that point and is not obligated to continue. In the event of termination by Totally Divine, this company agrees to return all materials related to the project to the client in a timely manner.

11.   Any dispute between the parties arising out of or in relation to this Agreement, or any breach of this agreement, shall be mediated by a mediator from the King County Dispute Resolution Service or other mediator as agreed to by the parties. The cost of mediation shall be shared equally by the parties. Either party may initiate mediation by written notice to the other, and mediation shall take place within thirty (30) days of such notice.
        If mediation fails to fully resolve the dispute or conflict, the remaining dispute or conflict shall be settled by arbitration pursuant to King County Mandatory Arbitration Rules or another arbitrator as agreed to by the parties. Either party may initiate arbitration by filing a complaint with the King County Superior Court, and the prevailing party shall be awarded costs and reasonable attorney's fees. Venue for any action shall be in King County, Washington.

12.   Any notice given hereunder shall be in writing and be delivered or mailed by Certified Mail, Return Receipt Requested, to the addresses set out below.
        This Agreement is entered into on this first day of February, 2011, in the City of Seattle, the County of King, and State of Washington.

Appendix B: *Rooted in Water: The Gullah Geechee People Script*

Rooted in Water

The Gullah Geechee People

Setting the Stage – how it was

DVD 1B Chieftess of the Gullah 2.15 (Singing)

My spirit calls out. My spirit calls out. My spirit calls out to Thee.

My spirit calls out. My spirit calls out. My spirit calls out to me.

They tried to break my will by taking me across the sea.

They tried to break my will by taking me from my family.

They tried to think that they could take what God had given unto me.

But they only rooted me deeper in the spirit you see.

My spirit calls out. My spirit calls out. My spirit calls out to Thee.

My spirit calls out. My spirit calls out. My spirit calls out to me.

Awaken this day and begin a new start

That can take all things but your soul and heart

These belong to me, you are my art

We are forever joined, thus will not part

My spirit calls out. My spirit calls out. My spirit calls out to me.

VHS 5 122.20 QUEEN: we're going to do our libation right here 123.12 DRUMMING...GREETINGS, WE'RE HERE TO POUR LIBATION...NAMES AFRICANS CALLED GOD...WHEN WE POUR LIBATION WE POUR IN REMEMBRANCE OF GOD...REMBRANCE OF OUR ANCESTORS...THEY MAKE THE PATH FOR US TO BE HERE...THOSE OF YOU WHO ARE HERE NOW...FOR THE CHILDREN...FOR THE CHILDREN WHO ARE NOT YET BORN....WHO WILL COME AND LEAD US TO TRUE FREEDOM...LOOK TO THE FOUR POINTS...NAME OF SOMEONE WHO REPRESENTS SOMETHING POSITIVE IN YOUR LIFE 125.15 WHEN I LOOK TO THE EAST I REMEMBER THOSE AFRICANS WHO BE TRAVELING...WHO BE CALLED SAMURAI...AFRICANS COULD GO UNDER WATER AND KEEP THEIR EYES OPEN...ASHE...126.08 NORTH...GEORGE MOSES HORTON....FIRST AFRICAN POET...NORTH CAROLINA...SPOKE OF FREEDOM...WHO STILL HAVE THEIR 40 ACRES AND A MULE...ROOSEVELT GAVE THE LAND BACK THAT THEY DESERVE 127.09 SOUTH...SHIP CALLED INDUSTRY....BY AMELIA ISLAND...ANTELOPE BEFORE THERE BE AN AMISTAD....NEVER GOT THEIR FREEDOM...SAVANNAH....WEAVED THROUGH CAROLINA....THE WANDERER CAPTURED JUST BEFORE THE CIVIL WAR...128.26 WE LOOK TO THE WEST...GERMAN ORIGIN...ABOVE SAVANNAH...BEHIND A MAN CALLED SHERMAN...EBENEZEER...LEAVE THOSE AFRICANS FOR THE CONFEDERATES TO BE KILLED...GAVE US 40 ACRES AND A MULE...DIED ON THAT CREEK....WE MUST HAVE OUR OWN...130.25 QUEEN WHO SACRIFICED HER CHILD FOR THOSE PEOPLE TO CROSS THE WATER...131.18....[NAMES CALLED OUT]...133.12 DANCING AND DRUMMING...138.41 AMEN. ASHE...

VHS 5 138.52 Queen: There is nothing by accident...7 number of completion....139.30 We are not here in this circle by accident. All of us were here to complete this...we were needed to complete this...it was divinely ordered...to say at this moment in time...I'm going to plant something in their spirit and it's going to be up to them after that...140.40 the weeds choke the plant that you're supposed to eat later so that's why you can't let others wind up their roots around you, you have to know what your roots are...so there is no accident. Everything is for a particular time and for a particular place...142.30 weeds...don't let them choke out your harvest. And a lot of us don't know how to reconnect to the soil and the soul and the land that we grow from because we let other people choke out our roots...we know about the field...

VHS 5 136.29 [SINGING] OH FREEDOM...BEFORE I'D BE A SLAVE I'D BE BURIED IN MY GRAVE...THEY'LL BE SHOUTING OVER ME...

VHS 6 38.06 Queen:...this land before was not called Carolina...indigenous people...every brick made by the Africans who were kidnapped...forced to protect the British...they're owners were paid because they were rented out...red tone because blood was in those bricks...not just military but spiritual fortification....you had the knowledge and they were telling you you were nothing...Osceola...head was shipped up north to study his brain size...excellent strategist....42,18 do not respect enough to spell name correctly you can figure how they treated him when he was alive...

DVD 1D Queen: 55.20 we all supposed to minister...Saul was the name that he was given at eight days old...Gullah Geechee watch their baby for a week or so...they get a second name...59.00 they gave him...that paper name...being in bondage, most of our ancestors have that paper name...59.40 community name...Queen Quet...

VHS 4 Amil: 10:45 Heritage House...replica of hermitage plantation mansion house...when the government built that house they were letting us know... 11:25 we were still supposed to be captors...I don't use the SL word because that's like profanity to me...our ancestors were captors...the hermitage plantations are known for these bricks...rare bricks...there's a hefty price for them...they will steal the bricks...the people who made the bricks were African people...

VHS 4 24:48 Amil Jamal Terre: Cooper river area...combine all the works of African people...that work would be greater than the great work of the Pyramid of Egypt if you put that work together and that was done by Africans...that was not dealing with the other areas...in that one area of South Carolina where you have about five rivers going through...25:58 [Ancestor voice] the African was brought here for the trinity...what be the trinity? ...cotton, rice, and indigo...the genius of the African be the trinity...the African genius for sugar cane...

VHS 5 143.06...we developed all of what you call America...if it wasn't for the sell of us...you wouldn't have this....Liverpool England doesn't come unscathed...their foundation came from the sale of black cargo...their intention was never for us to be standing here like this...I have a choice whether to let somebody else put me in bondage...I can put myself in bondage....I can always be free....it's on me but it don't control me...chain your mind...don't want to admit you're in bondage of your own...

VHS 4 47:59 Queen at fountain...steam ship...48:19 a lot of Gullah Geechee does not feel they have any attachments to England however ...Liverpool was one of the main ports where ship building was done before they went around the coast of Africa and enslaved Africans...would take a negro that was there to pay for their trip...would end up at port is Liverpool England...best places to go to learn about Transatlantic slave trade is Liverpool England...black cargo which is us...when you see the thinks at this historic sites it's interesting what's written and what's not.

DVD 1D 5.46 Amazing Grace...John Newton was a slave carrier himself...he was the one who wrote that...in Sierra Leone when he was captured by Africans himself...being in bondage himself could he hear the spirit speak to him...we now sing as if it were one of our spirituals...took ownership of it...take ownership of what Paul is saying here in this letter to the Corinthians...

VHS 4 102:37 Queen Quet: [ancestral voice, pumping water]...indigo...use baskets and sweetgrass...103:24 this is a place of work, not play...baseball is a popular past time to the Gullah/Geechee people...en route...Amazing Grace Lane...Leroy Brown...this baskets has colors in it...traditions keepers...106.14 music for us here...Gullah/Geechee people...was very key as to how the work was going to get done. The plantation here is a task system which meant you had one thing to do in the course of a day...how many volunteers I got? None! You don't work, you don't eat...107:37 You don't have your own well, you in trouble...salt water...chemical from golf courses...pollution in the waterways...this is why it's important to have your own pumps. 109:04 Forty acres and a mule...civil war...self-sufficiency 114:29 PEOPLE GETTING WATER...115:23 when that person's pumping the water, somebody else might have to hold the weeds out in the field, somebody might actually be picking the beans...and they were doing all those things...the person that would be setting the pace would set to certain songs...115:54 *WORK TOGETHER CHILDREN, DON'T YOU GET WEARY...MEETING IN THE PROMISED LAND...PRAY TOGETHER*

*CHILDREN, DON'T YOU GET WEARY...MEETING IN THE PROMISED LAND...*117:20 SHORT HANDLE HOE...WORK TOGETHER CHILDREN, DON'T YOU GET WEARY...They attribute that the Gullah/Geechee invented the long handle hoe because they're the ones out there working....118:57 people now live in at 16 bedroom mansion and don't want two people in there because we no longer work together... Carolina gold...*WORK TOGETHER CHILDREN, DON'T YOU GET WEARY*...fan outside the house...no volunteers again! Have more of an appreciation next time you eat...we figure out a way to make it with some rice...122.14 When you eat something from now on you don't just think it grow on a plastic bag anymore...

Land Ownership

VHS 4 11:25 the first railroad system in the US was on the hermitage plantation...our ancestors were working it...our ancestors were operating it...12:40 that's a part of our history that is uncovered when we begin to look...but we got that house smack dab in our community and again a sign and those are the things we can't let permeate us...black folks have owned land since the 1700s, since the 1800s and it is still here and this is sacred soil that we're on...

DVD 1B 7.02 song created in these plantations...*Children of God keep on marching...one of these days you should be free...Keep on marching...one of these days you shall be free...*

VHS 4 107:37 before the emancipation proclamation, Gullah/Geechee became the first African people to become official landowners in this country by paper because all of this area had been confiscated...all the Caucasian people had abandoned it and all that they had, including us, was to be sold...... deeds remain legally...name...everybody was listed on your deeds back then...why to try to force people to try to find a weak link in families today who may not have been raised here but are heirs, to try to get them to be convinced that what they have down there is not worth nothing...money took was 1/10 of the value of the land...that's why I do the work I do every day to educate people about their land rights, their human rights, and to educate even those who are away about the value of things here...

VHS 6 113.53 We got on this soil there was no easy time....going from the point of being the cargo to being property owners...how can you give away a legacy?...

VHS 5 133.51 CHANGE IN DRUMMING...134.11 RATTLE RESPONSE...

VHS 3 305:20 SIERRA LEONE...IS ONE AREA...THE RICE COAST...LARGE NUMBER BECAUSE OF THE RICE PRODUCTION INDUSTRY...THOSE WERE SOME OF THE MAIN PLACES WHERE WE WERE KIDNAPPED AND CAPTURED FROM...COMING TO THIS AREA? CHARLESON/SULLIVANS ISLAND 306:27 CHARLESTOWN WERE ALREADY ESTABLISHED...OVER 40% OF ALL ENSLAVED CAME THROUGH SULLIVANS...307:10 ENSLAVEMENT SHIPS WOULD BE DOCKED IN THE ATLANTIC...BOATS USED TO....FERRY OVER...LARGE FLAT BOTTOMED WOOD BOAT...BLACK CARGO 307:52...

VHS 5 43.49 we begin at the beginning...paying respect...indigenous people who were here before Africans brought her...Sullivans...not by accident that we have a reunion here...we gather...because you should start at the beginning...45:00 creek blood...Seminoles...Seminole wars...46.16 we pay homage here...indigenous and enslave them in the Caribbean...we have to know that the things we look at as monuments are not there by accident...we are not here by accident, everything is divinely ordered...whenever we pay homage with respect...these physical thinks can always be taken away...

VHS 3 249:09 INDIAN HILLS...THERE IS ALSO AN INDIAN MOUND...INDIGENOUS WERE ON THIS ISLAND...DIFFERENT INDIGENOUS PEOPLES BLENDED...CALLED SEMINOLES OR AFRO SEMINOLES...OKLAHOMA, TEXAS, OUT IN MEXICO....OLD GULLAH (OLD ENGLISH)...MIXED WITH MUSKOGEE...MEXICO...SPANISH GULLAH...BUT THAT IS STILLPART OF OUR LINEAGE AND HISTORY AND OUR HERITAGE AND CULTURE AND WE KEEP THOSE LINKS...

DVD 1B 11.22 95% of white people in Charleston got some kind of black blood in them...not admit that though...

VHS 3 259:56 BLENDED NOW...NO RESERVATION...ISOLATE THEM ON THERE AND STARVE THEM OUT...COME TO MY HOUSE...NEVER ABLE TO ACCOMPLISH THAT GOAL...INDIGENOUS AMERICANS SLAVE...SEMINOLE...EXILE AND WILD...SOME OF THEM DID INTERMARRY...THE GULLAH WAR...MORE NEGROES IN THE WAR THAN ACTUALLY INDIANS...HISTORY OF TODAY IN THE CONTEXT OF TODAY...

VHS 6 103.08 Queen: Sullivan's Island...pestilence houses...black cargo...put you in bondage...if you had too much of a strong will they had to break it first...walk across hot cobblestones to be sold at market just like they sold...all the other work tools...when we come to these islands we come in respect of our ancestors...of all that they went through...in order to give birth to scientists...

VHS 4 124.25 [REENACTMENT]...Amil...prayer....those that prayed flat down in the wilderness...and when you hear...that tell me what clan you be...majesty of the lion...we be lion...we be of the family of those the power and glory...the Africans that come here first...Hilton Head...then they come...those Africans travel on up the river...128:42 What be this strange place?...this place feel like home...but this place never be home!...'I will follow me'...we keep the genius of Mother Africa... 133.21 they still have freedom on their mind...

The Genius of Africans

VHS 4 Amil: 32.16 Africans, when they came here, they were scientists, they were astronomers that they were able to plot the sky with their naked eye...didn't need the telescope...that's all a part of the genes...

VHS 4 Amil: 28:47 in certain parts of West Africa they had 25,000 schools then Nigeria had 3,000 schools...Africans didn't know how to read and write, that's a lie, that comes from afrocentrics, we wrote and still had the ability to tell our story orally...you see them writing in Arabic...

VHS 6 222.00 one of seven Muslim people...222.17 we still pray to the east so that's probably the Muslim influence...a lot of people still don't want a woman to be the minister of the church...woman and man always separates...

DVD 1C Amil: 6.00 CLAPPING...shout comes from...the shout comes out of a movement that...counterclockwise...tied to the hajj...we are supposed to go to Mecca...African Muslims...one thing they couldn't do, they couldn't make the pilgrimage to Mecca...around that which was sacred to them...doing a shout...Christians but foundation out of Muslim experience...the things that you do are directly tied to your African/Muslim ancestors...

DVD 1C Amil: 16.42 we are a people of land and a people of water. Overriding all of that is the spirituality...

VHS 6 29.09 CEREMONY WITH QUEEN & DRUMMING...30.27 PROCESSIONAL WITH DRUM 34.45 *BEFORE I BE A SLAVE I'LL BE BURIED IN MY GRAVE AND GO HOME TO MY LORD AND BE FREE.*

DVD 1C Amil: 4.19 [BEFORE I BE A SLAVE I'LL BE BURIED IN MY GRAVE]...tied to people....a spiritual song based on what people experienced [FREEDOM], out of those Africans with traditional beliefs...that's a part of your foundation...

Spirituality

VHS 3 237:17 SINGING
WHO'S THAT YONDER DRESSED IN WHITE?
I WANT TO CROSS OVER TO SEE MY LORD
IT LOOKED LIKE THE CHILDREN OF THE ISRAELITES
I WANT TO CROSS OVER TO SEE MY LORD
WHO THAT YONDER DRESSED IN RED?
I WANT TO CROSS OVER TO SEE MY LORD
IT LOOK THE CHILDREN THAT MOSES LED
I WANT TO CROSS OVER TO SEE MY LORD
WELL WHO THAT YONDER DRESSED BLACK?
I WANT TO CROSS OVER TO SEE MY LORD
IT LOOK LIKE THE CHILDREN ARE TURNING BACK
I WANT TO CROSS OVER TO SEE MY LORD
          ??? JORDAN ???
I WALK ACROSS TO SEE MY LORD
VHS 3 239:00 NATIVE SPEAK. (COTTON, RISE)
VHS 3 240:30 CLAP...IF YOU WERE FROM HERE I WOULD HAVE KNOWN BECAUSE AS SOON AS I BEGAN...YOU WOULD HAVE SPOKE...I HEARD ONE OR TWO VOICES...THAT MEANT THEY WERE RESPONDING TO THE CALL....WE STILL USE THESE PRAISES HOUSES...1850S...EVERY PLANTATION HAS ONE...

VHS 5 153.21 how do you think we know all about this? The spirit. Once you're walking in the spirit you're basically walking in the spirit...look in the air asking...go to bed with it...walk right to it...just like any type of medicine...your natural genes...

VHS 4 134.17 Trail of Tears...134.45 no man own their soul, only God only their soul... ...136.04 we still knew where our souls were centered...137.06 when they were marching...they would have to be Catholic first...they didn't have to convert, they could continue their language and praise and worship that is Gullah/Geechee...

DVD 1C Amil: 12.07 Gullah/Geechee...we are still African people...we are the synthesis of all that which is good...13.40 religion/spirituality...it is an integral part of the culture...when the Africans came over...understood that God helped them to survive so they were not gonna give up on them...God continue to guide them...practice them to seeking...seeking in the wilderness...

DVD 1C Amil: 9.22 you're Baptist or you're Methodist because when the Africans came here they would go to the water...baptizing people in the water...so Gullahs would do something...940 because in Africa, at home, we understood the connection between water and spirituality, so we would go into the water as a part of our spirituality, we would go into the water as part of our celebration...water represents spiritual purity......so when they see the Baptists are...they became Baptists so they would still be connected back home...and so that's what they were doing...10.25 you're ancestors chose this particular way because it was a way of survival....still to maintain that connection to Mother Africa...11.34 to try to get some of the eyes to open up where they're no longer blind, where they no longer have the hard heart 11.47 we come into the house of God through different doors...

VHS 6 115.23 *OH I COME THIS FAR...AND I TRY THIS FAR...MY JOURNEY ON....YES I COME THIS FAR...*118.56 BELL RINGING...WALKING ONTO THE BEACH...AMIL with basket on his head 122.46....REENACTMENT....TRYING TO BREATHE SOUND...DRAWING IN THE SAND...123.14 Amil: give thanks and praises...Africans that pray...in the wilderness...we remember those African souls of those nations. AHHHH. 124.21 God almighty sent me here to be with you...I traveled from the south....124.58 Horn sound...blow the conc shell...see African man like you because we all come from Africa...smell like home...taste like home...make this be like home...I will follow you...I will follow you...128.12 don't you see the boat!?! 129.58 Charleston...Africans who fight for freedom...Haiti, the first African nation... 132.15 FROM A DISTANCE, COME UP ON THE 'INTIMATE' GROUP 133.37 Amil: look down from heaven and say you want that woman to be your mother...Mother Africa sees the goodness in you...you must see the genius of Mother Africa ...we will now pick up the fruits...let them get their feet wet like we do back in the day 134. 30 tamberine...135:45 PEOPLE WAK OUT INTO THE WATER...138.35 DANCING 140.41 BIRDS FLY BY...WATER RUSHING OVER AMIL IN CHARACTED BOWED DOWN IN THE WAVES...141.09 AMIL WALK AWAY 141.27 DRUMMING IN CEREMONIAL AREA (FLAGS)

     VHS 5 48.30 when we gather here we let the drums resound...then we make our way to where the Africans went...50.30 DRUMMING AND CLAPPING 51.41 These drums come from Africa...they're human drums...communicate 100 miles / hour...when drums were taking away we use our hands...the purpose of clapping is to raise the spiits...53.38 DRUMMING & CLAPPING

     VHS 5 145.23 Queen: the heartbeat is our first drum...that's why we must reconnect to the souls in this soil to keep us on point...to keep us in sync with one another and the energies out here...there's balance...living land ways that's what it's all about...you cannot recreate this environment anywhere else and try to get people to understand...they have to feel it, they have to experience it...146.45 strength comes from the soil...cos we know it's not us...there's a higher plan...148.07 Gullah Geechee are oral people...148.21 share your thoughts, your growth...what your role can be in making sure that the nation is always here. 149.06 DRUM WALK BACK

Creative Action – How it is

VHS 6 110.10 what do you use for baptize...bring ancestors over here...clean out your body...can't live without? WATER! ...we pour in remembrance of God...we say Ashe...we pour in remembrance of ancestors....113:45 names of people of positive energy you want in this space...Ashe...113.29 ancestors whose names we can no longer call...moments of silence...Amen and Ashe

DVD 1B 18.44 Libation – tribute to our ancestors. Peace and blessings. Peace! We don't poor libation like other people...to honor the Africans who traveled here and came together...our way...water to the ground and say Ashay...when Africans poor libations there are four reasons why...in remembrance of God...the ancestors...the adults who are here who are present...the children...we poor libation in remembrance of who we come from because without them and without God we would not be here today...made it possible for you to be here today...our way, our family way...21.14 We poor libations for the Africans...25.13 South...Jacksonville, North Carolina...those who are Gullah/Geechee, you are God's anointed people...the first Africans to be in this country we call Gullah/Geechee...we are now in the sun...in the remembrance of the people on this very land...those Africans who fought for freedom. 27.27 Your own person who means something to me...29.19 to all those names we can no longer call because we don't recall...we still remember you...Ashe...moments of silence for all that we are together...we continue to ever be connected.

DVD 1B 42.44 we need to go back to old land mark...anytime we gather together is an opportunity to praise the most high for the continuation of us being here...so that our next generation has the werewithal to carry on because we have all this land to protect and if we don't teach them how to fight and hold on it will sure enough be gone...

DVD 1B 30.14 clap and sing: *Oh Freedom...should my Lord have me free...be a slave...buried in my grave...there'll be shouting...there'll be shouting over me...go home to my Lord and be free...Oh Freedom...[clapping]*

DVD 1A 20.05 the purpose of the Gullah/Geechee Nation is to institutionalize the culture...International University of Gullah/Geechee Nation...

DVD 1D Elder Carlie Towne & Elder Halim Karim Gullahbemi 22.56 GG Foundation...23.11 bridge between the people – foundations...23.42 seven part program arts, rep of people...your expressions as a people...stories, those ways...24.24 Maintain our identity...24.58 Work with young people...crafts and folklore...

VHS 6 142.30 elder c. towne / minister of information for the gullah geechee nation: greetings...welcome to the gullah / geechee reunion...thank you to come and celebrate your ancestors and your heritage...we love you because you be we...we be gullah geechee anointed people....to celebrate our(3) ancestors...because they died for us...that we may have the freedom that we have today...143.30 the gullah geechee nation has a mission...144.03 the mission statement...we are the gullah geechee nation, not an organization...144.20 the mission is to preserve, protect, and promote history, heritage, culture, language, and a homeland. to institute and demand a recognition of governace. the rights necessary to accomplish our misssion. to take care of our community....i am just a reflection of you...so the efforts will provide a healing environment and care for a well-being of each person of economic empowerment because what we have...we can connect the dots we can have much more just sharing and networking....145.55 Please understand that we are the link to our ancestors [drumming]...

Defining Gullah Geechee & Their Use of Language

DVD 1D 32.22 Nation is really about self-determination...maintain those traditions...maintains morality...ethics...holds community together...so other things that divine us can be circumvented by knowing who we are...35.15 we all connected.

VHS 5 154.15 we all basically from Africa...we all may scatter but from travel time we still got a connection...

DVD 1B Amil VHS 1 Amil (153.39) we are not meant to be sufferers...we become homogenized...we just become Americans... (156.35) 54.45 those are still children of Africa...you still have to go home...go back to your roots...you may not know where you are from specifically on the continent but there's a range...there's a cultural unity even on the continent...you can still find your way back...and you still see your foundation and that can then awake you...not logically possible for you to say I'm trying to find out who you are...fool, you're an African in America...

DVD 1B   15.30 slave relics museum...our ancestors were enslaved African people, some of them were even enslaved indigenous American people...we want to conquer this land, there were people already existing on this land...when our ancestors came together with the people of this land they then joined many of which we call today Afro-Seminoles or Seminoles are out West...they still speak Gullah/Geechee but they don't realize they speak Gullah/Geechee...those ties and connections...Oklahoma...Mexico...dispersed in various locations...Juneteenth...it is out of respect for our roots that got this far away...honor Juneteenth....18.24 giving praise and thanks to the most high and ask that all of our ancestors be at peace with all that we do.

DVD 1D 26.40 symbols to rep we as a people...create a flag for the people...27.26 People in a tree, rep a tree...on indigo...blue people...canopy is green – agriculture part of who we are as a people rep life...28.09 Once we had a flag...28.50 doing what we doing...head on our body...the people became a nation...we always was we just forgot...29.12 Queen Quet to carry the word...signed petition...29.53 in 2000 enstooled Queen as the head – write a constitution...council of elders wisdom circle...

VHS 6 Queen Marquetta Goodwine / Spokesperson for the Gullah Geechee Nation...scientist...computer specialist...historian...147.27 Queen: every year this time we gather...the first Sunday that follows July 2nd...hung for a plan to take Charleston....black majority would take the West...July 2nd I was enstooled...148.55 the interesting thing....how do you all become a nation? God made us a nation. God gave us the authority...God gave us the authority...look on top of things...look on the surface...there's a lot more underneath...

VHS 4 53:40 Brother Amil Jamal Terre, very conscious, committed brother...54:24 God...gratitudes...honored to have one of our own...she follows in that mold of those people try to guide, trying to enlighten, trying to inspire...she is my sister, this is Queen Quet. She is the Queen because she works diligently for Gullah/Geechee people, for African people...she came across the water...

DVD 1C Amil: 34.50 Geechee...were people that were from West African...fight against the bondage...folks come here...they come Geechee...become Gullah...they're African people...racist folklores...who have said things about us...trying to tell people who we are...they had a genius within them so they brought the Africans here...36.29 there's no distinction of who we are...we define who we are...then tell us who we are...self-determination...we define ourselves...be addressed accordingly...37.13 that's what we have done in Gullah Geechee...

DVD 1D Queen: 15.10 Modern Pharisees...school doesn't teach about Gullah Geechee so they can't exist...ancestors charge you to carry on..15.35 We are the children that are to come...someone in word going through what you feel you going through....16.06 History repeats itself until we get it right...17.07 *OH LORD DON'T TURN BACK...PRAY ON DO'T TURN BACK...FIGHT ON!*

VHS 6 249.14 Gullah people are the ones that socio-anthropologists, ethographers with this term for us in the Carolinas....and Sea Islands...academics came up with to fragment us...over the years the term Geechee was used to mean any backwards...rice eating Southerner...hold on to tradition....Geechee came from African roots...gidzi...rice cultivation...gola...Angolans...names got corrupted over time...gullah...buyer beware...Georgia Africans had to live and work more closely with Europeans than those in the Carolinas so we kept our language, we kept our traditions ...spiritual practices a lot more firmly...now....more Africanisms...Geechee which is our bridge language...252.36 but when you live this, there is no distinction because we can understand each other even when others don't understand us...

VHS 4 4:58 Queen: Goose creek is where strawberry... where the Gullah Geechee still are and where they spread their seed...historians come here don't look at connections and the interrelations across the boundaries from one state to the other but they stop at that line...

VHS 3A 43:11 QUEEN: ... For all of us who are Gullah/Geechee, we know that we travel by the water...people look at it now by the mainland so these State boundaries are the boundaries that we need to be bound by and as Gullah/Geechee people we are not bound by those, we are bound by the Spirit and the Spirit has lead us to know and always remember who we actually are. They are one people...but then there is so much more to it than what they see on the surface and it's really about where your heart and soul are...and so we know that no matter what they say in terms of boundaries all of us are one people...

VHS 3 221.45 IN NORTH CAROLINA...they moved to the mainland because they could no longer maintain control over their island cultures and communities...when you had the onset of Jim Crowe...still recall making cast nets...but a lot of their language are not there because they had essentially been assimilated for survival purposes....

VHS 3 243:35 THIS IS THE GULLAH GEECHEE NATION...STARTS FROM NORTH CAROLINA...TO AMEILA ISLAND FLORIDA...JACKSVILLE TO JACKSVILLE....30-35 MILES....WHEN YOU UNDERSTAND WHEN WE TALKING LIKE THIS...WHEN TALK TO ENGLISH SPEAKING YOU DON'T END UP HEAING GULLAH YOU HEAR OUR BRIDGE LANGUAGE: GEECHEE WHERE WE BORROW WORDS FROM YOUR LANGUAGE TO TRY TO GET YOU TO UNDERSTAND WHAT WE'RE SAYING IN CONTEXT. GULLAH IS A LANGUAGE

DERVIED FROM ALL OF THOSE LANGUAGES FROM AFRICA THAT THOSE PEOPLE SPOKE 246:01 CLAP...SPIRTUALS...THEY'RE CALL AND RESPONSE...SENDING A MESSAGE...

VHS 3A 44:34 CB: We're almost like a people with two languages. For ourselves we talk one way and for outsiders we talk...dot our Is and cross or ts...

VHS 4 212.58 we have to speak the King's English...because it's the dominant language...when we hear anything that does not sound English, it's different and in the Euro-centric way of thinking...difference means it is either bad or good...different can't just be different and leave it alone...depending on a Euro-centric construct...

DVD 1D QUEEN: ...reading in 2nd Corinthians, the third chapter...41.55 read it our way, you should be able to turn to....verses -6 then to verse 12...45.12 once we are able to articulate the things that they'd be able to use in this region, we'd be able to better serve...why didn't you just say that? 45.55 us wanting others to make things plain is not new...one man wrote 2/3...49.50 not that we are sufficient...use great plainness of speech...we were backwards or ignorant...go to school and learn to speak proper...what is proper in one...is considered improper in another culture...you're in another place now...to the Queen what Americans speak is improper, so who is the judge?

DVD 1D Queen: 00.59 some of these folks...the elites...Pharisees...wanted to look at the letter of the law...no matter what the law book say...ready to kill that person because they weren't just doing what they knew....even though God had given me this tongue to speak...we be anointed people...been in a different place...be satisfied where you are and then study to know what you're here to contribute...Paul was sent to a religious school..plenty of books...what subject are you looking for?...written in your own language...our language is oral...what language isn't oral?...about paper = it can burn...book burning...couldn't burn people hearts...chains...Jesus was born in Africa...

VHS 6 150.30 proper is about whether you're doing it right or not....When I've gone to Britain darlings they don't think you speak English at all...so who's doing the judging when we use words like that? It's because we use words like that that we use many...

VHS 6 253.28 we help people...it is okay to speak your dialect...not sland, not ebonics...this is a dialect that reaches back to Africa...reeducate the community it's okay to be who you are don't apologize for who you are...it is the linkage that keeps our hearts and spirits indebted to Africa...this is a celebration that we still exist and we must connect from coast to coast 255.50 who speaks for we, we speak for we 256.45 freedom ain't free and I will not compromise it...we were chosen for this work...this is the work that the Creator has chosen for us and the ancestors have assigned to us...

I am a Vessel

VHS 4 Amil: 04:40 as I tell people the story of our history it's a weaving, it's a fabric, and we just have to know what we're dealing with...

VHS 3A ALLIANCES 42:05 besides the one in South Carolina you don't have another recognizable Gullah Geechee community because it takes a while for black people to find themselves and recognize themselves as such...almost you got to go in and pat them on the back and tell them who they are and then they're kicking and screaming and denying ...yea we are a special people and we are a bit different and we should go and find that difference instead of being ashamed of it. So right now...only two entities actually embracing it...

DVD 1A 09.38 Young black males being arrested...how positive for this event can be for a young person to learn consciousness...avoid some of this negative behavior. 11.16 They're like Queen, we never knew our culture had all this history...and now they feel they have a duty to educate other brothers not to go the path they took because there's so much more they could be doing with their skills to build a nation. 11.50 Ask the people outside of here what are they doing to help the Nation?

DVD 1C Amil: 26.16 something that resides within you...I'm a vessel for my ancestors, for my people, to tell their story...that is still what has helped African people because we've still been able to carry on the culture [YOU TOOK ME, YOU TOOK ME WITH YOU]...they're with you, you just have to listen to them...when you hear certain words it strikes your soul...help you identify with who you are truly...

DVD 1B Amil Jamal Terre / Elder Gullah/Geechee Nation / Georgia and South Carolina 47.34 It began...when I was five years old...I understood that I was African, and a lot of that was tied to my family...the first human beings are from Africa. ...that's us...and that created the drive and the passion within me to know who I am and who my people are....to understand how special we are...interest in history...the genius of Mother Africa that remains within us 49.27

DVD 1B Amil 56.30...make sure that the young people around us know who they are but also the other adults because sometimes it becomes when adults don't have understanding and think that they're impacting wisdom when they're imparting madness...

VHS 3A 22:43 to this day old people refuse to speak up because they don't feel they get any results...That's why so many young people speaking up because...It's still in their mind that they cant get anywhere so why say anything...22:57 So we're down to one community now and we're struggling to hold onto that community because that's the only place that isn't developed. Now we're under pressures from the State, from developers...that is probably the only place we own ourselves...23:12 People wonder sometimes why you want to hold onto something that your people struggled and died...but that's exactly why we want to hold onto it. 23:25 This is the last true Geechee community in Georgia because of the isolation...over the years if you spoke the Gullah/Geechee language you were forced to speak about that language.

DVD 1C 17.09 Amil: I always strive to cover my face...let it come out of my mouth...that's what you're taking...it's about the message...what I'm saying is the most important thing...causes me to be humble...trying to transport you...back to a particular place, to a practicular time... [WHAT BE THAT STRANGE PLACE? THIS PLACE TASTE LIKE HOME...FIGHT TEETH AND NAIL TO MAKE THIS PLACE HOME] even for just for a second...the living history...is to tell the story of the African people...I'm going to touch people...I want people to understand...[YOU BE A PART...]

DVD 1A 12.09 Imagery and how that affects your mind...the long term range...having positive images on your walls, in your house, to counteract the other stuff they put on the internet...46.44 imagery...the art of success...that represent us as humans and our connection to nature...to raise funds for the nation but to raise awareness and to always uplift the minds...54.15 the generations...you have to teach them, train them to be responsible....54.57 we've got to have the faith that we are powerful enough to stop it if it just takes one person...55.15 as African-Americans we have to put a stop to America destroying our young people

VHS 4 31.33 here in Savannah we have our monument to African people...my concern is that it really doesn't reflect us, or reflect us in a certain state or reflect us symbolically that needs to be tweaked, but it's good that we do have a monument that acknowledges us...41:40 Queen Quet: that's why the person that's gone through your living experience cannot truly interpret and project your experience and that's why...having a monument that's supposed to be celebrating the evolution of the African in America and their survival as a family unit, I don't see why the family looks downtrodden, why they have chains at the base of their feet when they're wearing modern day clothes...as you try to walk forward those chains are in front of you...they think that it is minor things but if you live that culture it becomes momentous. 43:00 Amil Jamal Terre: with that particular monument...controversy...first image it was decent...done by a Caucasian, it had them together....looking at each other...chains unbroken because it was around that time around emancipation, no where do we go from here? Then discussion later on...then the images change even more...

VHS 4 157.18 Millennium Monument...seven of these...unveiled in 2007...3D monument...158.31 pulling up a portion of the world...pulling up Africa...other continents inside of it...this is his bloodline that goes into it...and goes back into where the different children...158.55 next side of it...weight of the world on her back...birthing position...that bloodline...it's all connected...the last view, the nature view...nature even looks at you...so whatever we're doing to nature it's doing back to us so if we take care of nature...with all of these you see that it's all interconnected...200.03 European Struggle...you should be able to see yourself in all these things...pulling down from his head because all struggles begin in the mind...you see the turmoil can come from outside or from within...201.36 Gullah Geechee success project...placard with a sentence of empowerment that the nation has created...

VHS 4 101:48 Queen Quet: Images at home are critical to the growth of our children and about what their thought patterns are going to be later on in life...102.13 so it's very central what seed you plant even to the eyes and the ears.

DVD 1A 13.14 importance of adults having the responsibility to carry on...keeping the Nation alive...How are we going to make our adults accountable for teaching our children about our history, about our African nation? 13.46 First off a lot of adults don't even know our history...just because you were born black don't mean that you know black history...somebody still had to still show me...what the children must know you must teach them. And the you meaning any of us who are adults. You can learn from anybody...our biggest problem is that people have told us that we don't have anything to offer each other but that was a lie...14.39 we need to recognize that we have so much skill and ability that that was why our ancestors were kidnapped in the first place...they were being hauled over here to work for free. We have to know that history ourselves and respect that work ethic is a good thing.

DVD 1D 7.26 some of us are overlooking our resources right here in our own community, our elders ...they don't have a Ph.D...but guess what they got...understanding...so much wisdom...so much knowledge...we were so persecuted because we used to treasure our elders and respect them....8.06 a person could be your elder in two minutes...don't follow me down this path...9.05 being disrespectful cos should have listened to what we told them...9.22 a lot of these things we got away from in our community we should have never gotten away from but we thought it was improper to...it wasn't proper for them because they were not tied to a legacy of Africa that has these traditions in them...10.30 there are some things you don't need to buy...somethings because of our teaching we believe we should do...

Seeking and Rite of Passage

DVD1D Queen: 100.50 Mother raises the son for the first seven years and the father and the men of the community raise him for the next seven...what happens after that? His rite of passage because he's supposed to be able to contribute to that community as a man does...so these are traditions that some of us still maintain, they're not all gone... 101.40 there are some things that we study that we need to go back...people start to attack one and question your authority...

DVD 1A 17.50 rites of passage with males and females...it was modern day...but there were things that I had to do...okay now you are a lady...seeking...we really need to go back to even if we evolve it as a rite of passage...skills...survival skills that are traditional skills...you can survive....it's a matter of other groups emulating and keeping it up...all of us haven't forgotten...being a support system for each other...support that rites of passage...rules and regulation...if you don't start it at birth, how do you think that somebody at 20 years old that they gonna do it...

DVD 1C Amil: 14.28 seeking is directly related to...young people in the wilderness...to become members in the community...you must go seek it in the wilderness and you will go get a spiritual parent here...the white cloth around your head so that people would know that you we seeking...in west Africa...religion...is a part of the culture because it manifested in the things that we do...table tapper in the church...in the praise house became the communal place for us...your equal say...to deal with spiritual issues...and the secular issues...integral part...cannot separate it...spirituality is a part of our life blood.

VHS 3 241:30 ...PRAISE HOUSE WAS OUR CENTER...OUR PRAISE HOUSE IS WHERE WE WOULD CONFIRM THAT YOU HAD DONE THE SEEKING...MEANING YOU WOULD BE CONSIDERED AN ACTIVE PART OF THE COMMUNITY BECAUSE YOU KNEW RIGHT FROM WRONG BASED ON WHAT WAS CORRECT IN THE COMMUNITY.....

VHS 4 152.50 So you can maintain these traditions but you can also evolve those traditions...153.14 zoning maps...cultural overlay district...153.30 Most of our Sea Islands our cultures have been sandwiched into...Saint Helena...because of the laws...154.44 International...Gullah Geechee University...classes...workshops...quilt...everything is done by hand...156.16 having to tell them our story...something that looks simple like a quilt is not the simplest thing to do.

VHS 5 52.38 Carolee Brown/Quiltmaker – inherited from my grandparents...and I just decided to go ahead and make some...I make quilts that are heavy that's going to keep you warm otherwise I'm not going to waste my time making it to look at or hang on a wall. QUILTING AND WHAT"S INVOLVED 54.04 once you catch on it's pretty easy...this is just like a hobby for me. 54:41 TRADITION? Has always been cos all of my grandparents made quilts...I'm the only one of the six that make quilts...the others are not interested...but if I give them a quilt of course they'll take it 55.21 FAMILY ART? It's not an art, I just pick up some material and cut it so...[SHOWS ONE SHE'S PUTTING TOGETHER]...57.17 granddaughter...oldest daughter, she can do it but she is busy...GENERATIONS BACK? 58.00 neighbors and friends would get together and sit and sew...nobody accompany me...58.42 I just watched...my mother in law used to make quilts...how she does the tie...if you mess up anything it's gonna be yours...59.29 it might look like an art but to me it's getting some material, putting it together and sew...it's pretty easy...100.30 I line it with blankets...100.,56 I hope to see it continue seeing that my granddaughter is interested...101.25 QUILT WITH TIES...102.55 Carolee Brown: 104.04....about 2-3 women between here and Bufort....104.26 marquetta, she is the one who has totally got me back into quilt making...I had thrown it away...I have to thank God for her and that I can still do it...when I don't want to clean my house I can sit and gaze at the television and sew...105.04 has this class...I think then some of the younger generation will catch on and do it...because the younger people like to sit anyway...they can put a quilt together in less than a week...that's what I call fine art when you see her work. ORIGINATED IN THE SOUTH 106.12when I grew up everybody made quilts because you had children, you couldn't afford to buy blankets so they made quilts to keep us warm...106.36 it originated here because we didn't have central heating...10749 sewing class and television...this is what I think some of them do...its not hard...it just takes a lot of your time sitting and making you crazy...108.12 ANOTHER QUILT...MORE QUILTS...ABOUT FOUR TOTAL

Legacy & the Museum

VHS 4 57:32 often talk about what people are not doing but we need to talk about what they are doing, especially if it's positive...old land law and build each other up because that edification of the spirit is what has kept us here and what's going to take us into the future...well definitely in the name of our ancestors we give thanks for them...58:49 email from brother from Somalia...Queen of the movement...Slave Descendants hold on to their heritage...and they were proud that we were holding it down...59:50 the power of that has life there because you have the breath in it...59:59 we think we can do it all on our own...I'm FROM an island, I'm NOT an island...

DVD 1D 30.41 every year we have a reunion...31.06 All year we're going things to raise awareness....31.17 we got a great response from community because we all know now...31.31 Foundation does and see whose working to rep their ID and we support that...doing things our ancestors did, the legacy of it...

DVD 1A   04.10 Rivers of Storytelling – share our own stories...our own stories...[language]

DVD 1A   04.33 We want you to tell us what that museum should represent for people of African descent in the Americas...DVD 1A 04.47 Unlike other museums where they fix it, put it in your community, and tell you what your story is, this one we want the community to tell us what the story is.

DVD 1B 9.01 heritage tourism is worth money now...

VHS 3 226:04 Queen: On Hilton Head...what they were going to do to reclaim our story, reclaim our position here was to start a celebration of who we are...annual...celebration...throughout February...recognize the presence of the continued existence here...They go out there thinking they're going to be entertained and they're really out there to be educated.

DVD 1E 31.35 you don't get to do everything you want to do in order...with restoring old buildings you have to come in and document the building which is a year and half process then its time to raise the funds so there's many layers to try to get something restored...the projects that will help the society the most to bring the people...32.25 in a small town the biggest obstacle is funding...on a national level, what they want to fund...they're going to give money to something that's going to bring them attention...33.36 more in the sense of preservation, there's more controversy around that...when you talk about setting up ordinances...libertarian street...people don't like to be told what to do...Charleston was the first city in the United States to get a preservation ordinance in the 1930s...it's not only important to preserve our culture but in the sense of tourism dollars and it's a quality of life issue....37.12 It's not just lets go out and restore this building...so it takes a long time you know...see a need, get it down on paper, then go after the money and go on and doing the project...it's about people who will spend money...aesthetic work before the structural work first...

DVD 1B 33.45 they are the last hold out...of the Gullah/Geechee...original houses...restored...living history...so that people know the stories of that part of our nation...how they lived...survived...continued to be there...continued to hold on to their compounds...you don't have to go to the island to find family...who you represent in the nation....true blue Nubians...where your roots at?

VHS 7 203.20 The legacy...known as the Borough...the way of life...how they were displaced...there are at least two buildings remaining that represent what was...I would like the legacy to live on...

DVD 1E 16.00 Queen: pieces donated...kept in the family, as people can get a visual image of what went on here cos the house was completely empty...quilts...patchwork...ties...topstitch...there are no closets, a closet is a room...taxed you on every room in the house...17.58 southern belles....20.00 people think the plantation story is the story that they seen in Gone with the Wind and they want that version of the story...historic workshops...are all the patches that have to come together, for the whole story to have to come together to be seen...this place was on the Maye River...22.12 it's always key to see ships, that we have to remember the same kind of boats would make then used to take people and bring them here...23.40 infantry...Harriet Tubman...she thought it was barbaric and she too was of African past...sit under those oak trees and she started feeling those spirituals and they became part of her soul, part of the fabric of her being when she realized it was not barbaric....

DVD 1E 39.43 Queen: house on the waterway...in order to try to get the house...this property could remain so future generations can know the stories here...come to in journeys...Oyster factory alive...as part of our continuum, as part of our tradition...last four oyster factory...55.22 Queen: where people keep tradition....individual pier...individualism...and then people are no longer connected like they used to be...it's really ironic to see the journey over time...56.21 ironic of the boats going out...area where Africans were enslaved...57.11 folks...are only thinking about themselves...when you have a situation like that....traditional...it's a new form of segregation...for us it's about the group, it's not about the individual.

DVD 1E 59.59 QUEEN WALKING TO THE BOAT...Chains to lock things down...need to secure it...the irony of still having chains...the age that's on these chains, this is really another dynamic...tone that's not different than my own...and seeing the red on it....the blood that had to have been on the chains of our ancestors...imagine having to be on the water...they secure items now that can't talk but we were items that could...but they never asked us a question.

DVD 1B 40.10 it is wonderful to be in this space...and an appropriate to tell our story and to show things that our people have contributed even after breaking out of them heavy chains [broll] we just have to break the chains off of here now and that's choice...41.10 if they can endure all they did wearing a 100-pound ball chain on their ankle, why can't they do it now just because the air condition broke in your car? ...we get so comfortable now...remember all of what has happened before we arrived because everything didn't start happening when we each were born...plenty that went on before any of us even arrived and we need to have the utmost respect for all the others have even endured...

Tour of the Land

VHS 3 253:19 WANT TO GO TO A BEACH...BUT DIDN'T REALIZE HOW MUCH HISTORY THERE IS ON EVERYWHERE THAT YOU'RE WALKING...NOT JUST KEEP THE HISTORY TAUGHT BUT WE PROTECT ALSO THOSE THINGS THAT WE LIVE IN BALANCE WITH WHICH ARE OTHER CREATURES THAT LIVE IN NATURE. 257:21 OSPREY NESTS...ENDANGERED BIRDS...WILDLIFE PRESERVE...GULLAH OSPREY...LEARN TO SHARE...95% OF THIS ISLAND IS STILL GULLAH GEECHEE OWNED...HUNTING SEASON...TOURIST SEASON...

VHS 3 247:17 ONE THING WE DON'T DO IS BUILD OUR HOUSES ON THE WATER...BUILT IN THE MARSH....SEA ISLAND ARE BARRIER ISLANDS MEANING WE PROTECT MAINLAND AMERICA...SO THAT MEANS IF THESE ISLANDS ARE DAMAGED OR DESTROYED, EVENTUALLY WHATEVER HAPPENS HERE HITS YOU SO IF THE WATERWAYS ARE POLLUTED...IF IT KILLS OFF ALL THE SEAFOOD...SO THEY DON'T UNDERSTAND WHAT GOES INTO IT SO YOU CAN HAVE IT...SO TODAY AS YOU TAKE THIS JOURNEY WITH ME THROUGH THIS ONE PART OF THE NATION...READY?

The Importance of Water

VHS 4 18:43 Amil Jamal Terre: ...come to River Street...walk down Bull street..we all would sit on the water, we would sit...just be talking...it was probably something that was spiritual with us, and it was tied to our ancestors as part of that journey. 19:57 If you're going to have a tour of Savannah you must begin at the water, Savannah is tied to water. Savannah is a port city...mother city of Georgia. 22:00 Hutchinson Island...came up river and began to let our people off right here...This is our beginning, the water is where we come from...still trying to escape...some hope of freedom...

VHS 3A 117:59 Queen: The water that bring me is the water that might take me back. So we believe the water is what brought us here. So for us the water is about nurturing, it's about healing, it's a passage way. It's not something that you play in or play around with. We find enjoyment but it's a rejuvenation that we get from it and fulfillment that we get from it because it cleanses the body and removes the toxins and it allows us to reconnect and reattach with all the Spirits we know for us are out here in these waterways....So for us water is our bloodline because our blood is connected in to it.

VHS 3A 121:26 ANCESTORS WHO ARE BELIEVED TO TRAVEL BACK TO THEIR HAUNTS ACROSS THE WATER: One of the reasons why we always say 'the water that bring me is the water that might take me back' is that if you notice in our burial...we bury such that the feet will face toward the water and we bury on the water, we generally don't bury inland...so that way when those spirits rise, they rise and can immediately walk back home and home being the Motherland that we call...that people today call Africa...to reconnect with that spirit energy that they came out of...and ultimately to the creators energy as a whole. So for us it is very significant being on the water in this realm of life but on the next realm of life and so we believe our ancestors do walk back. Part of our ancestry is ebo...and several of the ebo people that came here and refused to be put in bondage walked back even with the chains still on back through the waterway and we believe they walked back to the Motherland, back to Africa...

VHS 3A 123:11 THAT WAS THE LEGACY OF EBO LANDING? There were many ebos that were brought into the Sea Islands...and then they were later taken from the auction blocks...Saint Simons...once they were there they refused to remain there and so many of them walked back with their chains on....childrens book...people can fly...these were Gullah/Geechees who commanded their spirits to lift from the earth and then took off in flight and flew back to the Motherland instead of walking...Because people were more intuned with the earth that they could command from the earth...God tells you that you can tell the mountain to move and it will even move but that's about the faith and that's about the grounding to be able to command that type of thing to happen that logically that you don't think is possible...for a lot of people they want to relegate the stories of the ancestors to being legends to the past and not realizing how connected it is to their present and how knowing those things can take you firmly into the future.

VHS 3A 9:56 BEHAVIOR CEMETARY...(story...community nearby called Behavior Community...taking glasses from headstone) 11:30 making medicine, ropes out of it...11:58 the red bulbs...get it off the tree...footstools always toward the east...so their feet is always toward the east...we always said back to the Mother Land. 12:37 We originally had 44 families on South Sapelo, we now have 7 families.

VHS 6 206.45 our spirits still walking among us...where most of our people grow up at...still feel a spirit presence on that end of the island...so we believe in spirits. No ghosts, just spirits....

VHS 3 227:43 Queen: I can hear all the voices of the ancestors crying out...it's a painful thing to experience...they're going to rise up again and what other people recognize as a hurricane is going to wipe out a lot of what they see.

VHS 3A 118:43 Queen: Whenever I come to the Atlantic Ocean then I always give thanks to those that are in that waterway still because their bodies remain there. To sort of giving peace for them...whether its for them to stay connected enough to speak back to us whether its through that sound in the conc shell...the waves...so whenever I go out into the water I first give thanks to the Creator for allowing me to be able to hear and still touch...and get power from this energy that's in that space. And so then to give homage to all of my ancestors who are still in that space and then to ask for the energy to come forth and go on into the next journey. ...Give prayer for the right energy to be conducted into the remaining meetings of the day because those meetings are key to the survival of this particular community and so that's one of the things that I do anytime that I come close to the Atlantic ocean and can touch it and have it touch back my hand as well.

VHS 3A 120:18 CEREMONIES PERFORMED HERE? The Gullah/Geechee people are not ceremonial people, they're not ritual people so they don't go and have things that are centered among all of us that we do. There are things that we bring out and place near the water...there are other things that do happen of significance in the waterway but not something that is timed or dated that has to happen...it's a place that we do respect for all that it's given us and all that it continues to give us because it feeds our body...we are a big people on seafood...so for some that might seem ritualistic but for us it's just realistic, and it's just a connection part of life.

VHS 6 259.18 Hunting Island...take a break from work....for the family, community...cross...first ships that started bringing our ancestors out here was named after Jesus...300.50 land seem it's reclaiming itself there...one up the Creator...302.15 North Carolina to Florida...ran to Florida for freedom...Great Depression...overt racist...304.11 people don't want to bring out the bones in the community...306.10 end up in Jerusalem...this was a sacred space to place himself in...American beach...

DVD 1E 14.00 we didn't know we were poor until we left the islands...what they meant by that was cash poor...they also had spiritual wealth because they were not putting all the time into just getting some money...14.30 even these spaces remind us of how far we've come...and yet there's still so much that we have to remember in order to know where we can go next...[CLAPPING] 15.00 the shout came out of all of these different kinds of edifices...they're painful to have to touch, your ancestors had to be strong to endure and still be able to create the spirituals...it's really an interesting space to be in...

DVD 1A 25.33 what is that you were looking for? You were looking for money...focus in your heart is into money...chasing money because you wanna buy a house, they need some land, they need a place where they can feed their family. Who in the Sea Islands don't already have...26.39 we have land here so fertile we can cut the grass outside right here and now...throw a few seeds...something's going to grow...just naturally because the ground is so fertile here...26.50 these other folks coming in here to try to put us out...they're coming here because this is where the gold is...this is where the diamonds are... ....but this is the diamond and goldmine right here: the land.

VHS 3 213:46 Queen: many of the people...lost their land...speak any language you translate ideas from one language to another, you translate concepts, you don't use words verbatim...so people who were not literate were approached by English speaking people who would come in with briefcases of money...I just want to use your land...for us something to generate the harvest and share it with me...turn their land rights over to another person...approached to joining property islands...intimidate and turn over...younger people sent away to school so they could get more knowledge of the Western thought patterns but be able to bring it back and transmit it to community, those people weren't aware people passed on and they were an heir to some other property and got lost for non-payment of taxes...not knowing their own land rights...cannot expand when God hasn't made any more land to expand onto without taking someone elses land

VHS 6 238.07 Quet: The journey today was like going back 200 years in time because what we're doing today has not been done by anyone in this area to recognize the connection between this area – Savannah, GA – and Africa....239.27 our ancestors were that connection so we had to pay homage to them...240.30 not having a fence up...something that is sacred ground for us...is not something to be privately owned...we are no longer someone's assets to be bought or sold.......selected and elected...but I cant do it by myself that's why there's a council of elders...246.18 I don't think the Creator's going to make any more land because we were created to keep the land, maintain the land...not to do with it whatever we saw fit and regardless of who else it effected...246.50 everybody wants to be a leader until you realize a leader has responsibilities...can teach me...and teach you...we are stronger together than we are apart....247.12 now we have to pray a lot more...shout a lot more...realize that a trick was played on us and we don't need to continue to keep the game going....and we need to work together to carry those plans out...

DVD 1A 27.58 we need to educate our people...on what land really means and that is our surviving grace as Gullah/Geechees....our ancestors...they had so much insight through being so spiritually connected to the earth they enough to put in them contracts everybody who wasn't even born yet...we don't need to give it away now......

VHS 5 111.48 QUEEN: This is P- island, this is....smaller islands that sit outside of Saint Helena...you don't always have to cross the bridge...112.10 when we talk about living culture and living land ways this is one of the main points that I wanted to bring people to...the land that goes all the way back through here...lost the land gambling but no one knew the family knew...by this time the land had been gone...instead of saying something to the family so someone can pay the loan off...so you have some who can't even talk about...they can spit fire, they can just about pass out...because it was uncalled for...the P- signed...cousins were heirs too...not going to move down there...so they were given pennies...attempting building of a multi-million dollar development...PUD...one of the enemies of the Gullah Geechee Nation...so what that is is...114.48 When the civil war went to the auction got the deed...other side of the family didn't go, they already live there, we own the island, they didn't realize the value of a simple piece of paper. Why? Because that wasn't their culture. They didn't need a piece of paper to constitute a contract...you lead by example...we were taught when you know better you do better so you don't know something and build on it, progress with it, teach from it so that others can learn...115.49 You are heir to something you didn't put one drop of sweat into and you figure sell it. Don't matter if other cousins need to live there, sell it...116.08 too emotional...it's a racial issue...you have native Caucasian people on this island who can no longer afford to live here, their children will never be able to live here...what they did was turn it over to National Park Service...so that it would be around...as open space that everybody else can treasure...Then we still have to battle because of all the historic resources they don't value...the Park Service...they're letting the chimneys our ancestors built...graves where their bodies are buried...be dilapidated...Demolition by neglect...If ...Kennedy's son – God bless the dead – had his wedding down here...Cumberland Island...but it had a story before he had a wedding there. It had a story before he was ever born so that should not be what the island is known for, it should be known for the Geechees who were pushed off of there...118.20 so that's why

I teach...for my ancestors...because we want to make sure they never forget us...

VHS 6 150.00 BIBLE ON PODIUM... 153.35 You cannot one up the one that made us all...the Creator sits something right in front of me to share...Jeremiah 2:6-7,11. 155.23 where's the Lord that brought us up from the land of Egypt?...made my heritage an abomination...156.43 If we were brought from...Africa...to a land of plenty...we had fruit there of 157.46 and made my heritage an abomination...Gullah/Geechee is heritage....can't read it in a book and now what it is to be a Gullah/Geechee...158.50 that is an abomination, you're making it into something that it should not be...159.45 our ancestors were brought in here to be sold...all the generations to hold the land...and eat from the fruit there of...

VHS 5...120.40 as Gullah Geechee we got to treasure our land...121.02 this is not the dumpster...no respect because they don't respect the blood that went into here...121.10 this island was the first Native American reservation designated for this whole nation...pushed onto the island...assimilate...starve them out...

VHS 5 121.50 my grandmother could make pottery from this soil, taught her children, but when they went north they forgot...and now that they've retired they wished they remembered but that was because of our ancestry...that she knew how to do those things...to hold on to culture...

VHS 3 223:50 QUEEN: For those who were waking up now...made to believe what they have was of no value but that they should seek after another man's treasure and so those people are returning home...to relearn what their great grandparents tried to instil in them that their parents thought it was a new time and now they're realizing they were being sent away from the land of milk and honey...a lot of them now have returned to the land to replant their feet. With any kind of plant and you pull it up by the root...it may survive or it may wilt...It's a matter of personal souls, personal journeys...

VHS 6 257.36 Queen: People need to realize that there are certain tools that people who came before them created and ...pick them up and start digging, digging for truth...so much healing balm in them...that there is no way that any tree cannot be sustained by it...[ECOPSYCH TREE]...you must take care of the root to heal the tree...

VHS 3 211:47 QUEEN: Hilton Head...really stopped being called Trench island when the cash crop started to boom...cotton king...Hilton....long grain Sea Island cotton...because it was all about economy...and he really set the tone for the place...212:40 have about ¼ of it that is now Gullah/Geechee. 25-30 years ago 90% of this island was Gullah/Geechee...sometime the numbers are including people of African descendent which may not be Gullah/Geechee. ...Encouraging the children to come back home so that they can repopulate the island and hold onto the culture that remains here.

Journeying Through Maruice & Cornelia's Story

VHS 3A 5:40 QUEEN QUET IN BLUE ON WATER – headed to meridian Georgia...hammond community...long time activist...99% of island is owned by the Georgia Department of Natural Resources. 6:18: QUEEN: Where we're headed today is Sapelo Island Georgia. We're heading over from Meridan Georgia...Our host for today will be the Bailey family which they live in the Hog Hammock community which is the last of the five Geechee communities that existed on this island. And so Georgia Department of Natural

Resources owns 99% of Sapelo Island and the 1% that remains
is the Hog Hammock community.

VHS 6 208.54 SAPELO ISLAND SIGN...210.09 thomas
spalding...sapelo is known as nigger heaven because...he kept
them together...he was going to breed slaves...a little more
freedom on sapelo...211.30 we go through a lot to stay here
on Sapelo island...211.46 light house...1920...to bring slave
ships in...

VHS 3A 6:48 QUEEN: We'll be hosted today by
Maurice Bailey and his mother Cornelia. Cornelia is one of our
long-term activists that has held on to this community and has
held on to the culture here as the community has dwindled
down from about 100 people to 65 at this point in history. So
we will be spending time with them today journeying through
their story.

VHS 3 RETAIN CULTURE 39:44 Being hardheaded and
proud...you're fighting against keeping something you have to
be hard headed...she believe that is right then that's the
course she's going to take...

VHS 3A 34:29 Maurice Bailey & Cornelia Bailey...We
have been here for nine generations on one side and ten on
the other. I'm sort of the know-it-all in the community...so I
kind of busy being nosy...that's how you learn things. If you're
not nosy you don't learn...I store up facts...pass them on to
Maurice sometimes when he ask for some...the rest I hope to
write down some more of it...give lectures all over the
place...We believe in God, when we was going up we believe
in Doctor Buzzard and then we believed in the number
runners who was the Bolito man and so this was the belief of
the people. 36:18 God was for giving praises to, Doctor
Buzzard was for revenge...You didn't ask God for revenge and
you didn't ask God for money...we had these preachers that

said 'the root of all evil is money' ...and so they played the number racket to hopefully get a few extra to supplement what they're doing and what they have.

Relationship with the Land/Ecosystem

VHS 3 218:47 QUEEN: ...this is part of history...mote around castle, it's a continuum...as African people our continuum is to live and be thankful for what the Creator has given us and so it's open to everyone for us to share because we're only stewards and caretakers...

VHS 3A 32:35 QUEEN: oyster shells, sand, lyme, and water. This is one of the things that African people that were enslaved here and became known as Gullah/Geechee brought over in the belly of the beast, in the hull of the slave ship was this type of technology and a lot of indigenous Americans in this area also would use oyster shells...it's called cocina ...here it's called tabby where we use the oyster shells so we never throw things away, we recycle it all...

VHS 3A 26:50 GUY: mullet is important part of our history...people said they didn't eat mullet because it was a bottom feeder fish and it wasn't a good fish to eat so all the slave...got mullets so we learned to smoke it...dry that...and we still use that mullet today...so we made these thing...Walmart sell everything...(Bee)...made from roast bones...cut them in various ways...and made our nets out of them.

DVD 1D 100.53 Ras: We come to fish...pay thanks for that...this right here is life...101.55 This is as natural as its going to get...

DVD 1D 39.40 Queen: do you know how many people would starve even though ....you give them a crab net...can't even farm...so now you might have to go to somebody else or starve...how did it get there?

VHS 3A 30:30 GUY: One more, you said you can put it in your mouth…When you're out there you fish against time and tide. THROW NET. Time, weather, time of the year, the Moon.

VHS 4 247.07 …sea islands were a togetherness…helped to keep anything drastic from happening…when went fishing and shrimping on their way home every house they would drop off…all those things tie in with who I am and why I am the way I am…main goal in life is to survive and to see other people survive…249.45 Gullah Geechee philosophy is there is enough for everyone…the need not to have ownership over everything is another one.

VHS 5 248.10 a lot of countries, the oceans are over fished…people start eating crab…government play a part in it because they license them….kind of mess up the food chain 249.57 people used to eat seafood certain times of the year…

VHS 4 FISHING 226.11 problems that have arisen…depletion of the shrimp…blue crabs…overfishing has been one of the main reasons…time of the year that they're being caught…amount of people that are actually fishing…hands on information seen change…soft shell crab…majority are female right before they lay eggs…don't see how the State government could let this happen…money get is worth it?…local crabbers have seen a difference…peeler crab traps…male blue crab as a bait…shrimp…

VHS 6 152.40 People can take everything here we need to exist and they don't get fined. 152.50 you put concrete over everything that exists and you put them roofs with tar….as they get raggedy they fall off…wonder why you ain't got no crab season…

VHS 5 213.59 CREEK SERVED COMMUNITY? 214.11 it was everything…transportation…source of food…source of income...source of pleasure...it was pretty much...it was all they had...it was entertainment...it was everything to them...it was something that kept fathers and sons together...whole families...marsh good for livestock....

VHS 3A 28:20 LOOKING AT MARSH WATER 28:33 GUY: Everything feeds off that grass...that's why people don't want people developing the marsh...

VHS 5 215.21 How has it changed with all this development? You lose a good part of the beauty...of the nature...food chain is a little different...change of the channel....dredge for large big boats in from of their homes....

VHS 3 207:23 QUEEN:...looked down and saw purple ribbon in own color and took that as a sign chose the right place to stop in all the madness out here...I knew this island when it was two main roads...I don't know how many turtles are still alive here now...people who are interested in nothing but recreation here now, there's no regard for preservation there's no thought it seems to what was here before, what's here now, what's here outside of this gate...what else is outside...over there where are people are still living as well. And even knowing that there was so much more that nourished...until the pollutants came...people rather be flying kites rather than being grounded in all that they're walking over because there is so much blood...that I can hear that is crying out from this soil...Trench island...trench in war people dig and go down in some place to hide but it also means ...get caught in the trench not so easy to come up out of it....just imagine what my ancesters must have felt...cant see another shoreline...they surely must have felt like they went into a trench....

VHS 3 144:58 QUEEN: (GOLF COURSE) this area's has people that buy into that because they base it off the fact that they are ecologically sound, they are environmentally safe, that they promote wildlife preservation but the reality is, to create these golf courses they create them with chemicals, then you have to maintain them with chemicals they also now have to put other kind of chemicals down to make sure that the birds don't come down and feed here because they don't want the bird mess on the ground. This is very interesting, this whole mentality that goes into this design process.

VHS 5 252.26 Mother Nature has a lot of ways of calming things down...Mother Nature working real hard to try to get people to wake up...storm category five or six...after two weeks people went back to their own crazy ways...305.10 You can't beat nature but you got to learn to live with nature...

VHS 6 225.15 we love nature...we respect the earth...everything comes from the earth....we pick up sand...we believe in taking care of nature and we be taken care of...they know when animals are mating...

VHS 4 247.07 the first cowboys were mainly all Gullah people...they brought over their horse work...tracking and hunting...were sea people also...

VHS 5 154.50 already in the gene...could talk to the horses...genuine animal person...father did more of the creeks...now my uncle was a horseman too...we're more the ones adapting into the hunting world...we learn respect for respect for every living thing...you respect the tree...once you learn how the system work...

VHS 4 245.33 I love winter team as well as getting out into the country...I use my time out in the country to gather my thoughts...relate a lot of interaction between animals and nature to humans and seeing the way certain the way animals tolerate each other...humans should be able to get along...the dependency on animals to each other is similar to the dependency to humans on each other...

VHS 4 253.37 I think that's one of the things with the Gullah people to is we lost all connection with the environment which really was a beacon, it was one of the things that helped keep us down to earth when we saw ourselves as a figure in nature...as a part of nature as compared to now we've gotten into the ownership and we feel we're above nature which is totally wrong because we're part of the dirt that we walk on, we're part of the trees that we see every day, we're part of the plant that we take in every day...when we farm we help the plants to grow so when we get our touch from nature back then I think it'll help us in a roundabout way...

Direction Energy is Flowing – How it Shall be

VHS 7 01.50 Queen: always connected so always begin with council of elders and pouring libation with a circle...it reminds others we are always connected; we are all dots on that circle...2.25 pixel...you need all those dots to be in the right place to get a picture...302 we want to make sure that all of our ancestral spirits...give us their blessings...next generation so that they know who they are even in the midst of the concrete jungle...335 we came from forested areas...there's more health, there's more growth where you have trees and vegetation than there is in concrete...359 we have to stop, letting the Creator fill us with the right things at the right time. 4.21 Amil: as always...we pour libation the way we want to pour libation...we are a cosmology...we are a mixture of all African people...we pour in remembrance of God, the ancestors, for the children who are here...who will be coming here...we start with the four points of the Earth...8.49 you call those who mean something to you... 9.55 it is a blessing for all of us to be here...this is the place that the drum 10.40 we have to lay the flowers of the sweet remembrance

of our people...12.15 flowers out of palmettos...someone
who's not jealous of the craft, who wants to pass it on...13.35
OUR voice is being heard...

VHS 7 14.10 Queen: I remember having a vision to be
able to speak words to others along this coast...14.30 we are
proveyors of our story, we are provayers of our culture...so we
don't be lying to nobody, we tell you like it is, how it was, and
how it shall be...it has to happen in Divine time...15.55
celebrating the spirit, the words of the Gullah/Geechee
people...

VHS 3A 45:00 CB ...we're rich in knowledge and we're
rich in land and we're rich in knowing who we are and at the
same time there's a lot of things that we still have to conquer
and overcome.

DVD 1A 20.05 The Gullah/Geechee culture is good for
everybody...talking about getting back, we're going
forward...into the future, we can never go back to the way
that things were...

VHS 3A 135:54 WATER TO WISDOM...YEA...cos the
water has so many things and the more that you handle
it...things through the water, you handle the wisdom...Take
care of roots for heal the tree, you can't take care of roots
whether they are human roots or tree roots without having
water as well...or you dig up a lot of the roots of trees, you still
find that they have a lot of wisdom in them...*[sequoia story
water in roots Blessed Unrest]*...

DVD 1A 20.40 as a foundation we're the roots that
hold up the tree...20.52 take care of the root...heal the
tree...take care of each other...21.21 let's reason
together...21.47 each and every one of you can solve the
world's problems....the Nation has it in place...we will show

you what's going on and connect you so you can stay connected because it's about building for the future.

DVD 1D 1902 *I NEED YOU, YOU NEED ME...STAND WITH ME, AGREE WITH ME...IT IS HIS WILL THAT EVERY CREATURE SURVIVES, I NEED YOU TO SURVIVE... I NEED YOU, YOU NEED ME...STAND WITH ME, AGREE WITH ME...IT IS HIS WILL THAT EVERY CREATURE SURVIVES, YOU ARE IMPORTANT TO ME, I NEED YOU TO SURVIVE...*20.35 Somebody's having a little trouble in their life right now...sing these words right here...20.56 *I PRAY FOR YOU, YOU PRAY FOR YOU, I LOVE YOU, I NEED YOU TO SURVIVE...I NEED YOU TO SURVIVE... I NEED YOU, YOU NEED ME...STAND WITH ME, AGREE WITH ME...IT IS HIS WILL THAT EVERY CREATURE SURVIVES, I NEED YOU TO SURVIVE...*

VHS 7 29.15 Amil: Our purpose in being here is to pay homage...came through Savannah...York...Monrovia...then they were taken...we are here to pay homage to those Africans..this was where the quarantine station was....two story tabby structure...30.42 this is an African burial ground...they represent something else to us: FREEDOM. 33.00 Antelope was before the Amistad...flowers and fruits...cast into the waters...in remembrance of those Africans...35.09 Prayer...35.52 OOO FREEDOM...

VHS 7 *17.24 OOOO FREEDOM, OOOO FREEDOM, OVER ME...AND BEFORE I BE A SLAVE, I MIGHT BE BURIED IN MY GRAVE...AND RIDE HOME TO MY HOME AND BE FREE...CLAPPING...*

VHS 4 Amil: 27:28 our genius remains with us and it stays with us as long as we continue to understand that Mother African is there for us. Places...when you take that genius and you combine it, you begin to feel the love of our people...and then you feel the love of yourself so then you're never lost.

DVD 1B Amil: Get around those who are positive 58.30 there are those who will have an impact on your life who you may never call mother, daddy...impact on your life...and cause a ripple effect...who will then touch other people...we have to get back to using our common sense...58.58 they were honorable people...there are pockets...certain people who were honorable and we have to get back to that...59.46 with regard to young people...we will begin to the seeds, we will not know which ones will germinate but we begin to reaching out rather than just be within ourselves....be honest with self...100.21 we have to be about uplifting

DVD 1C Amil: 24.06 it can help you to begin to feel good...to feel good if you're Gullah/Geechee...then to if you are African then you know about the genius of your people...able to see a star that only last century was NASA able to show the world...24.52 I'm proud...then it doesn't become a struggle for me to define who I am or to determine what I must be about....what part of the genius...do I want to take it into the secular...spiritual...fighting for your people...uplift your people...or are you going to guide your people...the liberation of your people...

VHS 7 22.29 ISLAND IN WATER...ON BOATS...24.17 DRUMMING ON BOAT...UNDER BRIDGE...CLAPPING...26.10 CONFEDERATE FLAG....27.15 SINGING...'JOURNEY ON'...

VHS 7 44.20 African proverb...when you give honor to your ancestors, we will have success...They're telling us to take care of the future, don't forget the future, we must take care of the present and then we'll be able to move on to the future...

DVD 1D 29.14 IF YOU LIVE RIGHT, HEAVEN BELONGS TO YOU...[CLAPPING] HEAVEN BELONGS TO YOU...

VHS 7 59.10 PRAYER: God our Father...Thou who has brought us thus far on our way...lead us into the light...keep us forever in our path we pray...bless our feet...bless our heart...beneath our hand...may we forever stand, true to our God, true to our native land [TOSS FLOWER TO THE WATER]

VHS 7 100.20 *EVERY VOICE...LET OUR REJOICING RISE HIGH AS THE MISSING SKIES...LOUD AS THE ROLLING SEA...LET US MARCH ON...GOD ON OUR SIDE...*

The End – Credits

Appendix C: *Rooted in Water: The Gullah Geechee People* Documentary

Requests for the documentary can be sent to:

Tiffany A. Dedeaux
TOTALLY DIVINE
orders@totally-divine.com

About the Author

Tiffany A. Dedeaux wanted to redefine her relationship with the natural world after spending more than a decade as a video editor for various broadcast news departments around the west coast of the United States. It was as a video editor that Tiffany discovered her gift for digital storytelling and developed her heart-felt craftsmanship. She started Totally Divine Video Editing in 2000 as a creative outlet. Later, as a presenter and trainer for a couple of software companies, Tiffany discovered a desire to walk with people from the land of *not knowing* to one of *knowing*...

Made in United States
Orlando, FL
20 May 2024

47063162R00098